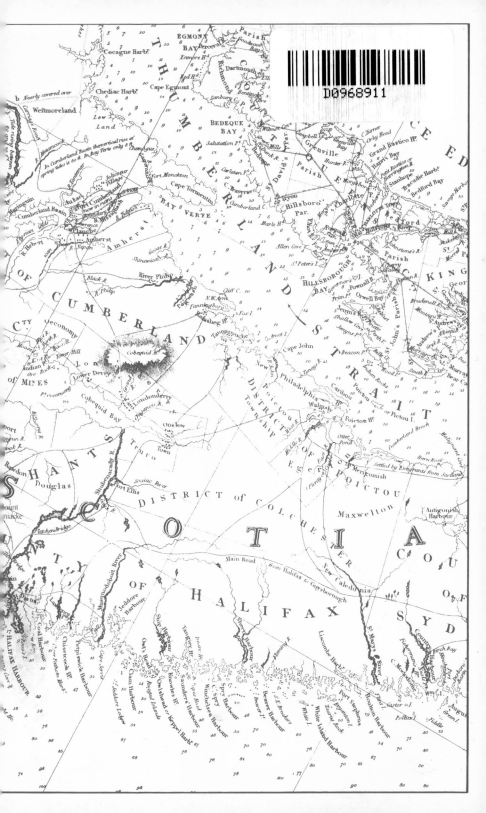

The Old Attorney General

By

Brian Cuthbertson

A Biography of Richard John Uniacke

THE OLD ATTORNEY GENERAL
— A biography of Richard John Uniacke 1753-1830

© Copyright Brian Cuthbertson

ISBN 0-920852-07-6

Published by: NIMBUS PUBLISHING LIMITED,
            P.O. Box 9301
            Station A
            Halifax, N.S.   B3K 5N5

Design: Promotional Print and Product Development Ltd.

Typesetting: Maritime Photoengravers Limited

Printed and bound in Canada.

Contents

Preface

Historians have been both fascinated and puzzled by Richard John Uniacke. Although he was unquestionably the most influential Nova Scotian in the first quarter of the 19th century and had, I believe, the most visionary and prescient mind in the British North America of his day, only one article has been published on his life. This was by the Hon. L.G. Power, whose paper on Uniacke was read to the Nova Scotia Historical Society in 1891 and published in Volume VII of its *Collections*. Power had to rely upon second and third generation reminiscences, Beamish Murdoch's *History of Nova Scotia*, and those official records he could locate. Uniacke's personal papers, which must have been voluminous, were destroyed after his death by a daughter-in-law doing spring house cleaning. The loss of those papers makes the writing of a biography, of what was certainly an extraordinary and remarkable man, a most daunting task.

Nevertheless, Uniacke's fifty years as a servant of the Crown in Nova Scotia has left its mark upon the public records and it has been surprising how revealing these records have proved to be. As a member of the assembly, its speaker, solicitor general, attorney general, governor of King's College, and member of the council at varying periods of his public service, Uniacke wrote much; some of it because of his official position as attorney general, but most of it in a lifelong effort to influence the British government to turn its attention to Nova Scotia and the other colonies of British America. What marks Uniacke out from his contemporaries is his vision of a British America as a great empire arising in the northern part of the continent. To achieve this vision he believed that the British government had to bring about a union of the colonies and invest capital so that the redundant population of the British Isles would flow to British America. These views he first placed before the British government as early as 1806. His 1826 Observations on the British Colonies in North America, in which he proposed a federal union, reads in parts like the British North America Act of forty years later.

Many have assisted me in the writing of this biography, but I owe a special debt to Professor J. Murray Beck, who has recently retired from teaching in the Department of Political Science, Dalhousie University, and to Majory Whitelaw, author and broadcaster.

This book is dedicated to Richard John Uniacke's grandson by the sixth generation and named after him.

Brian Cuthbertson

May 1980

Chapter One

Some Irish Recommendations

In the late autumn of 1774, Richard John Uniacke, aged twenty-one and not quite a year out of his native Ireland, stepped ashore in the old province of Nova Scotia. This was to become his adopted land. Here he would make his fortune; here he would become the most influential Nova Scotian of his time.

With one Moses Delesdernier, a trader of Swiss extraction, Uniacke had sailed a sloop (ill-named the *Hopewell*) from Philadelphia to Hillsborough, a landing place on the Petitcodiac River near the site of the present-day Moncton in New Brunswick. Repairs to the *Hopewell* had delayed their departure; as a consequence, they were still in Philadelphia when representatives of the American colonies gathered there for the first Continental Congress, a curtain-raiser to the American War of Independence. Whatever Uniacke thought of the rebels, he could not have foreseen that they would influence the course of this life in Nova Scotia, nor that the Revolution would have great impact on Nova Scotia itself.

At this time the boundaries of old Nova Scotia closely approximated those of the ancient colony of Acadia and incorporated the present provinces of Nova Scotia, New Brunswick and parts of Maine. The founding of Halifax in 1749 had marked Nova Scotia's real beginnings as a British colony. British settlements were at first restricted to Halifax while the Swiss-Germans were further south along the shore at Lunenburg. But in the early 1760's thousands of New Englanders moved north to the lush, dyked marshlands of the Fundy, vacant since the deportation of the Acadians in 1755. Others searched out the harbours from which they could engage in the lucrative bank fisheries. These New England farmers and fishermen established townships stretching around the south shore from Chester through to Minas Basin and the Isthmus of Chignecto. Across the Fundy twenty or so families settled along the Petitcodiac in Hillsborough township; others were further down the bay at Shepody and up the Saint John River. The first settlers, some eight thousand in number, were later joined by Scots at Pictou, Ulster Irish around Cobequid Bay, Yorkshire men at the head of the Bay of Fundy, and returning Acadians near Yarmouth and at the head of the Fundy. By the 1770's Nova Scotia was a cultural mosaic of scattered settlements surrounded by virgin forest and linked by water. There were only two roads that warranted the name, one from Halifax to Windsor, still very rough but over which carriages could be driven, and the other an offshoot to Truro. Although they were absorbed in settlement, Nova Scotians could not but turn an anxious eye to the upheavals in the American seaboard colonies from whence at least half of them had come little more than a decade before.

Uniacke had arrived in Philadelphia from the West Indies, having left his native Ireland in December 1773. He had been born on November 22nd, 1753 at Castletown, County Cork, the fourth son of Norman and Alicia Uniacke. His father was a prosperous member of the landed gentry and his Norman-Irish family could trace their roots back to Strongbow's invasion of Ireland in the eleventh century.[1] The Uniackes probably came originally from Brittany, taking their name from the district called after an Irish saint, St. Uniac, who had gone there in the 6th century. Family tradition, however, provides a more romantic origin for the name: it tells us that soon after the great Geraldine clan settled in Ireland in the 11th century, their chieftain was at war; a desperate attempt was to be made to attack their enemies through a narrow breach in a wall. A young knight by the name of Fitzgerald stepped forward and successfully led the assault. He was ever afterwards called "Unicus" (the only one), which was corrupted to Uniacke.

Certainly from the 13th century onwards the Uniackes were one of the most prominent families in County Cork. Staunchly Catholic, the family suffered much during the Tudor and Cromwellian repressions. Uniacke's great grandfather made a fortune in the legal work and bribery involved in the regranting of lands after the restoration of Charles II and seems to have been the first to become a Protestant. The family was bitterly divided over religion until the early 1700's, and those that remained Catholic again suffered as Jacobites when William of Orange defeated the Irish supporters of James II.

In the crucial Battle of the Boyne, Uniacke's grandfather, Captain James Uniacke, then a youth of nineteen, commanded a troop of King William's cavalry. After an arduous career in the army, he retired to a property near Youghal in County Cork, which he named Mount

---

1. For a genealogical and antiquarian study of the Uniacke family, see R.G. Fitzgerald-Uniacke, "Some Old County Cork Families — The Uniackes of Youghal", *Journal of the Cork Historical and Archaelogical Society* (hereafter *J.C.H.A.S.*), Vol. III, 1894 Nos. 30, 31, 33, 34, 35 and 36.

Uniacke. In the eighteenth century the family became as staunchly attached to the Protestant cause and the Hanoverian Georges as earlier they had been to Catholicism and the Scottish Stuarts. Their property now secure, they became the firmest of supporters of the Protestant Ascendancy in Ireland. Their patron was the Earl of Shannon, considered the most powerful politician in Ireland. Two of Richard John Uniacke's cousins held Irish parliamentary seats controlled by Shannon and two more became mayors of Youghal. Through marriage the family was related with Beresfords, who had in their gift one quarter of the appointments in Ireland in the third quarter of the eighteenth century. Uniacke's mother, Alicia Purdon, was descended from the Plantagents and came also from a politically influential Cork family.

Young Uniacke went to school at Lismore near his home until, at sixteen, he was articled to the Dublin attorney Thomas Garde. This was very much his father's decision. His grandmother Uniacke had encouraged him to pursue a religious life, but he had rebelled at the hypocrisy and rapacity of the Church of England clergy he saw around him.[2] A local Catholic priest became for him the only example of a pious and good man engaged in the ministry. Fearing that his son might be converted, his father decided to remove him from the influence of the priest. If he had converted, the iniquitous laws against Catholics would have precluded him from ever inheriting property or entering a profession, and would have ostracized him from his family. There was a rebellious streak in Uniacke's character; as his family would find out his departure for Dublin only strengthened it.

With its graceful Georgian architecture and the variety and refinements of its intellectual and social life, the Dublin of the 1770's was the equal of any of the smaller European capitals. The well-connected young Uniacke soon immersed himself in the political life of a city alive with the stirrings of Irish nationalism. Protestant agitation for the Irish parliament to have the sole right to legislate for Ireland was becoming more militant each passing year. Irish Catholics were finding voice in their struggle to gain relief from the penal laws that made them pariahs in their own land. The Uniacke family, as supporters of the Earl of Shannon and the government, had every reason to fear this new Irish nationalism. Their remembrances of past sufferings had instilled a fear of any political agitation that could lead to open rebellion. Much to the consternation of his father, Uniacke joined the ranks of the Irish nationalists. The result was a fatal break between

---

2. Uniacke to his son Andrew, January 10, 1828. Vertical Manuscript File: Uniacke, Richard John, Letters to Andrew Mitchell Uniacke, Public Archives of Nova Scotia (hereafter P.A.N.S.).

father and son.[3] His father ordered him to cease his involvement in politics; Uniacke, as high spirited and stubborn as his father, simply disobeyed him. In anger his father cut off his son's allowance and ordered him home. Uniacke refused to return and "in passion" decided "to seek his fortune in the New World".[4]

He chose the West Indies for probably no better reason than that an elder brother, Bartholomew, was stationed there as an ensign in the 60th Foot. He kept a journal of his trip from early December 1773, when he left Cork, to his arrival at St. Kitts nearly two months later. Here he first encountered slavery. He found it ridiculous that the Creole English, whose ancestors had known the value of liberty so well, should be instrumental in enslaving a race of people whose only crime was that "the same being which had created them...made them black instead of white yet with the same ideas (... when they have the opportunity of polishing themselves) that the English have of superior capacitys".[5] This perceptive entry in his journal was not merely the righteous indignation of a youth of twenty. His opposition to slavery was life-long. Thirty-years later, he was stubbornly attacking the whole system of slavery, arguing before a jury in Halifax in a case of a runaway slave that slavery in Nova Scotia had no basis in law.[6]

Not finding his fortune in the West Indies, Uniacke took ship for Philadelphia. As he was landing, Moses Delesdernier spied the tall powerful youth, obviously a gentleman, and accosted him.[7] Deslesdernier was seeking settlers for Hopewell township, situated around the Fundy marshlands of Shepody Bay a few miles down the bay from Hillsborough, and persuaded the young man to accompany him to Nova Scotia. Uniacke agreed to this, and to a proposition that he, Delesdernier and a John Moyes form a partnership to finance the

---

3. This and what follows is partly supposition, but see *Henry Morgan Papers*, Uniacke, 8099-8111, Letter "unsigned to Morgan, February 18, 1902, Public Archives of Canada (hereafter P.A.C.), "I have heard Old people say that he [Uniacke] has been involved in the political troubles which then ravaged Ireland".

4. Information of Richard John Uniacke in Uniacke versus John Moyes, Chancery Court Case No. 75, 1786. RG 36, P.A.N.S.

5. "Observations in the West Indies and North America", MG 1. Vol. 926, No. 97, P.A.N.S.

6. In an 1803 case involving a runaway slave called Jack, Uniacke told the jury "That it appearing in the Evidence that the servant Jack was a *Slave* and there being no slaves in the Province, the Plaintiff could not recover the loss of his Service". Joseph Alpin to Brenton Halliburton, November 16, 1803, MG 1, Vol. 334, No. 2, P.A.N.S.

7. L.G. Power, "Richard John Uniacke", *Collections of the Nova Scotia Historical Society* (hereafter *Collections*, N.S.H.S.) Vol. IX, p. 76. For Moses Delesdernier (1713-1811), see my article, *Dictionary of Canadian Biography*, Vol. V, forthcoming.

purchase of a sloop and trading goods.[8] Uniacke had no money, but managed to raise his share, £417, by drawing bills of exchange on his father. Still a minor, he must have lied about his age and used his natural loquacity to convince New World creditors to part with this sum.

Throughout his life in Nova Scotia Delesdernier involved himself continually in unsuccessful speculative ventures. He was agent for the Hillsborough township proprietors on the Petitcodiac and had been living in the township since 1765. Desiring to improve his circumstances, he had purchased land in Hopewell township at Shepody which had been settled ten years earlier by some twenty Palatine families. He owed money; his principal creditor was the lieutenant governor, Michael Francklin. When Delesdernier returned to Hillsborough with Uniacke in 1774, he found that Francklin had arranged under some pretext to have his house seized and was planning to have the Delesdernier family sent to Windsor. Delesdernier found other lodgings for his family in the settlement and immediately left for Halifax to placate Francklin, leaving Uniacke in charge of the family and of the sale of the trading goods they had brought from Philadelphia. By all accounts Uniacke proved "remarkably diligent" in meeting this responsiblility.[9] No doubt his legal training in Dublin stood him in good stead, but his inherent financial acumen was first demonstrated in that winter of 1774-75 in the settlements at the head of the Bay of Fundy.

In the spring Delesdernier returned from Halifax with the news that Uniacke's father had refused to honour his son's bills of exchange; Uniacke had thus lost his one-third financial interest in the Delesdernier-Uniacke partnership. It took on a new complexion, however when on May 3rd, 1775, Uniacke married Delesdernier's daughter, Martha Maria, not yet thirteen. Because of her extreme youth, a document was signed in which she agreed not to dispose, without her husband's permission, of any property that had been bequeathed her by her mother's family in Halifax.[10] Just why Uniacke should have married Martha Maria is a mystery. The marriage was probably not consummated for another two years, and when the Delesderniers and Uniacke moved to Shepody, Martha Maria stayed with her parents. Uniacke was an impulsive romantic and the

---

8. Information of Richard John Uniacke, *Chancery Court Case No. 75.*

9. Deposition of Joseph Lamb in John Moyes versus Moses Delesdernier and Richard John Uniacke, Halifax, Supreme Court, 1784, RG 39, Series "C", Vol. 33, P.A.N.S.

10. MG 1, Vol. 927, No. 4, P.A.N.S.

explanation for the marriage seems to lie in this facet of his character. It is unlikely he told his father of the marriage; the elder Uniacke would have been none too pleased to learn that his son had married, without permission, a virtual child who could not even sign her name.

In 1775 Delesdernier moved to his new lands at Germantown at the mouth of the Shepody River, and Uniacke went to live at Shepody Hill seven miles distant, where he attempted to farm. (This proved to be a lifelong passion with him, a hobby on which he could lavish some of his fortune). He had some knowledge of husbandry from his upbringing as the son of a prosperous landowner, but the young Richard John was ill-prepared for pioneer farming. The winter of 1775-76 was one of great hardship for him. In the spring he and Delesdernier attempted to renew their trading activites, only to have their sloop pressed into government service to supply the garrison at Fort Cumberland, which dominated the Isthmus of Chignecto. Fears were mounting: would the American rebels invade Nova Scotia?

During the winter Governor Francis Legge had ordered a mustering of the militia, but he had met with such opposition from the settlers that the order was rescinded. Half the people of the province were from New England and they were prepared either to support the cause of liberty or to remain neutral in a struggle which they saw as a civil war. Cumberland County, embracing all the townships at the head of the Bay of Fundy, was the most disaffected area in the province. Here Legge's attempt to call up the militia had been opposed by over three hundred New Englanders and Acadians, and even by some recently arrived Yorkshiremen, who had signed an address refusing to comply with his order.

Delesdernier, already singled out by the New Englanders as a loyal supporter of government, had watched with fear and anxiety the increasing disaffection in Cumberland County during the winter. Probably at the insistence of Michael Francklin, he circulated among the settlers of Hopewell, Hillsborough and Memramcook an address pledging loyalty to the King and the government which Uniacke and thirty-two others signed.[11] Delesdernier found himself further harassed for this act of loyalty and had good cause to fear for the safety of his family. In the summer of 1776 he brought them from Shepody to take refuge at Fort Cumberland. Uniacke with his wife joined them in a dwelling in the shadow of the fort, and the two men continued their trading activities.

Some Cumberland men had already gone over to the American

11. Petition is in MG 23, Al, Vol. 1, P.A.C.

rebels and were away seeking aid for an invasion force. Among them was Jonathan Eddy, who returned in the fall of 1776 with a ragbag force of seventy-two which he had raised from the settlements in Maine and along the Saint John River. In late October they arrived at Shepody and laid waste Delesdernier's property before proceeding to lay seige to Fort Cumberland.

Uniacke had not wanted to make the move to Cumberland; in fact, after the bleak and depressing winter at Shepody Hill, he had wanted to return to Ireland. He had discovered, not unexpedtedly, that his father "was much irritated against him for connecting himself with persons who were strangers to him".[12] His father was more than irritated; he had disowned his wayward son in the New World for having "highly disobliged him".[13]

Uniacke's impulsive nature now drew him into an association with rebels and a venture that was to end with his being charged with treason. It may well have begun as an adventure a year earlier, in 1775, when he travelled with companions to Pictou, following the trails down to Truro and across to the struggling settlement of fifty or so families of American and Scottish origin. The small American group was as disaffected as their countrymen in Cumberland County, and this journey may have been a means of making common cause. It was a thrilling experience for young Uniacke, tramping through the woods carrying his knapsack and cooking-kettle on his back and eating moosemeat shot daily by his companions. His association with the rebels ceased to be an adventure, however, once it became clear that Eddy's force was not the vanguard of an army equipped with artillery, but a motley crew enticed by dreams of plunder and with little hope of capturing Fort Cumberland.

The rebel weakness was not immediately apparent to Colonel Joseph Gorham, commander of the garrison, and his strategy was to wait out the seige until assistance arrived. He issued a proclamation for the militia to join in the defence of the fort. Delesdernier was one of the very few who answered the call. (He later claimed that both Uniacke and his nephew Lewis Delesdernier had accompanied him, but this was likely designed to disassociate any of his own family from the rebel cause.)

Delesdernier also took provisions to the garrison inside the fort, an act that enraged Eddy, who plundered Delesdernier's dwelling near the

---

12. Information of Richard John Uniacke, *Chancery Court Case No. 75.*
13. For the will of Norman Uniacke, see R.G. Fitzgerald-Uniacke, "Some Old County Cork Families — The Uniackes of Youghal", *J.C.H.A.S.*, Vol. III, No. 36, p. 247.

fort and threatened to deliver his family over to the Indians. A messenger was sent to the fort to get help, and Delesdernier, returning to his family, found them in great distress, subsisting on a few potatoes they had bought from the rebels. Poor Delesdernier was then captured by the rebels and forced to sign an "association" renouncing King George and pledging allegiance to the United States.[14]

Just what Uniacke was doing at this point is unclear. Eddy and his rabble were now engaging in the indiscriminate looting of the loyal, the neutral and even those who supported the rebels, and Uniacke was certainly no longer fully committed to bringing liberty to Nova Scotia, although on one occasion he did refuse to allow one of Gorham's messengers to return to the fort.[15] On the whole, however, it seems to have been fear of reprisals rather than any sense of commitment to the rebels which caused Uniacke to give support at all to Eddy.

There is a tradition that Uniacke played loyal to both sides.[16] He was probably as confused and uncertain as the Yorkshiremen and New Englanders, who were finding themselves overwhelmed by events. The garrison, shut up in Fort Cumberland by a force hardly more than half its strength, provided no protection against the intimidation and plundering of the rebels. The chief concern of the settlers was to protect their families and property. Once the rebels were defeated by a reinforced garrison in late November of 1776, the formerly passive loyalists took full, though short-lived, vengeance on many of those who had sided with the rebels by driving them out of the country and confiscating their property.

Uniacke did not witness these events. Some time before the successful attack by the garrison he was captured, under somewhat ignominious circumstances. He had met a Yorkshireman who was taking a load of pork in his wagon to the fort. Uniacke ordered the man to take it instead to the rebel camp, but found himself pulled off his

14. For Delesdernier's involvement in the rebellion, see the transcripts of General Sir Frederick Haldimand's papers in RG 1, Vol. 367, Nos. 13 and 14 and Vol. 367½, No. 51, P.A.N.S. The best history of the rebellion is W.B. Kerr, *The Maritime Provinces of British North America and the American Revolution.* (Busy East Press, Sackville, N.B., 1942). For a recent study of the rebellion in Sackville township see J.D. Snowden, "Foot Prints in the Marsh Mud: Politics and Land Settlement in the Township of Sackville, 1760-1800" (unpublished M.A. thesis, University of New Brunswick, 1974) pp. 88-127.

15. Uniacke told the messenger that Eddy would never forgive him and Delesdernier if he "imagine[d] they harbored any person from the Garison". Quoted from documents printed in J.T. Bulmer, "Trials for Treason", *Collections*, N.S.H.S., Vol. 1, p. 115.

16. Natham W. Marston to Rev. W.O. Raymond, September 4, 1889, Delesdernier Family, Archives, New Brunswick Museum.

horse and marched as a prisoner to the fort.[17] Rebellion was over for Uniacke. After Gorham's defeat of Eddy and his men, Uniacke and four other prisoners were sent to Halifax to be tried for treason.

Arriving in the wet cold of a Halifax winter, Uniacke had his first glimpse of the city that would soon become his home. It must have been a frightening experience for a youth just past his twenty-third birthday to be marched in shackles through the streets to jail. How much he must have wished he had never left the warmth and safety of home! There would have been taunts from onlookers no doubt looking forward to a public hanging. They were disappointed. Uniacke was soon out of jail and wandering about the streets of Halifax, the capital of what Edmund Burke dubbed that "ill-favoured brat of a colony".

Burke claimed (in 1780) that since 1749 the British government had spent £700,000 to maintain Halifax as a strategic outpost. Much of this largesse had found its way into the pockets of Halifax merchants and officialdom. Three or four thousand inhabitants huddled in shabby one-storey wooden houses from the harbour's edge up to the foot of Citadel Hill, living on British gold. Selling rum to soldiers and sailors was supplemented by the pickings of the whores of Barrack Street. Yet there were already men who were thinking of Nova Scotia as home, and even dreaming of a commercial destiny based on the fish of the offshore banks and trade with the West Indies. Merchants and officials such as Lieutenant Governor Michael Francklin and the meritorious Richard Bulkeley, the provincial secretary, had done much to keep Nova Scotia loyal by the judicious use of patronage, government contracts and a sensitivity to the fears and needs of the settlers in the outlying townships.

Uniacke's release was achieved more easily than a man charged with treason might have expected. Within the garrison there were officers who knew of the Uniacke family through his two brothers, then serving in the 40th and 60th Regiments of Foot. Two of his cousins had just been elected to the Irish parliament and other relatives were in the army. The inflexible Francis Legge had been replaced as governor by the easy-going Mariot Arbuthnot, who was under the influence of Francklin, Bulkeley and others such as Charles Morris, the surveyor general, and one of the two justices to preside over the trials of treason of the Cumberland rebels. These officials had no desire for vengeance; rather, they were determined to keep Nova Scotia quiet and loyal. Uniacke appealed to them, displaying full repentance and contriteness,

---

17. Howard Trueman, *The Chignecto Isthmus And Its First Settlers* (William Riggs, Toronto, 1902) pp. 233-4.

and using to good effect the prominence and loyalty of his family. It was not the last time that his Irish connections would come to his rescue, and no-one was more aware than he of their importance.[18]

An arrangement was reached whereby he would not have to face trial but would, ironically, become a witness for the Crown. Francklin most unfairly blamed Delesdernier for what had happened to his son-in-law and had him dismissed from all government employment for his supposedly disloyal conduct. The trials for treason of the others took place during the Eastern Term of 1777; all eventually either escaped or had their cases postponed indefinitely. Uniacke did not make a court appearance, but signed an indictment against two of those charged with treason.[19]

Not long after his release from jail he was in trouble again, and again taken into custody. This time it was for having failed to repay the advance on some hogsheads he and Delesdernier had agreed to provide, before his arrest. Although he seems to have had little difficulty in bailing himself out and settling the debt, his father-in-law was now both destitute and considered to be disloyal. Uniacke's own continued stay in Nova Scotia seemed unwise, and either on his own initiative or on the advice of others he made the decision to return to Ireland to finish his legal training. To raise the necessary money he arranged in August of 1777 for the illegal sale of his wife's property, worth £400.[20] Shortly after, he left for Ireland, leaving the pregnant Martha Maria in the care of her relatives.

Uniacke did not play even a minor role in the Cumberland Rebellion. What had probably begun as a youthful escapade had turned into a frightening experience. In the end fortune favoured him, but the ordeal left him much chastened and with a lifelong hatred of New Englanders, whom he reviled as "a race of the most lawless profligate and wicked monsters that exist [ed] on the face of the earth".[21] He himself never mentioned in writing that he had ever been in Nova Scotia during the rebellion. Of course Nova Scotians knew full well of his involvement, and the loyalists who arrived during and after the war used his revolutionary adventure against him in the ensuing vicious struggle for patronage. But he would become the leader of the

---

18. There is only family tradition and circumstantial evidence that it was his Irish connections that came to his rescue.

19. J.T. Bulmer, "Trials for Treason", *Collections*, N.S.H.S., Vol. 1, pp. 110-11.

20. Registry of Deeds, Halifax County, 23 August 1777, Vol. 15, p. 158. The transaction was later made legal, ibid., January 20, 1784, p. 197.

21. Dalhousie Papers, Notebook 1817-22. Anecdotes, A 537, P.A.C.

oldcomers, as the pre-loyalists came to be called, and triumph over his enemies.

Uniacke presumably completed his term of apprenticeship with Mr. Garde, the Dublin lawyer, and in 1779 he was admitted as an attorney of King's Inn, Dublin. Meanwhile his eldest brother James had succeeded to their late father's estate and likely made financial amends for the father's treatment of his fourth son. Indeed, his return to Ireland gave him the opportunity to rehabilitate himself with his family and their political patrons. None was more important than the Earl of Shannon, whose large estates in County Cork gave him control over eighteen parliamentary seats, including the two held by Uniacke's cousins.

The Ireland to which Uniacke returned was in the throes of change. The American Rebellion had acted as a catalyst to usher in an era in which the Protestant Irish sought free trade, constitutional independence, and legal equality for the Presbyterians. Uniacke was in Dublin during the great debate of 1778 which resulted in an act allowing Catholics to buy land and to bequeath their property as they wished. The Uniacke family opposed the measure, and the Youghal Corporation thanked his cousins James and Robert Uniacke for their "spirited perseverance in support of the Protestant religion" in parliament that year.[22] Uniacke, who later became the leader for Catholic emancipation in Nova Scotia, had by now learned the value of discretion, and would not have been open in his support of the act. The excitement in Irish politics continued, with the success in 1779 of the agitation to gain exemption from the navigation laws and allow Ireland to import and export directly from the colonies. This debate was Uniacke's first introduction into political economy; henceforth, he was a persistent advocate for the removal of those navigation laws that were so restricting to colonial trading.

In 1780 Uniacke went to England, where his Irish relations secured him an interview with Lord George Germain, the Secretary of State for the Colonies, who promised him the office of attorney general in Nova Scotia on the first vacancy.[23] With this promise and letters of recommendation from eminent Irish lawyers, he arrived back in Halifax early in 1781. When the attorney generalship became vacant that year, Governor Sir Andrew Snape Hamond thought it proper to let the promotion go according to seniority and appointed Richard Gibbons.

---

22. R.G. Fitzgerald-Uniacke, "Some Old County Cork Families — The Uniackes of Youghal, *J.C.H.A.S.*, Vol. III, No. 35.

23. Uniacke to the Duke of Portland, June 3, 1797, CO 214, Vol. 68, miscellaneous, P.A.C.

He appointed Uniacke in place of Gibbons as solicitor general at the request of Chief Justice Bryan Finucane. Hamond was not impressed by Uniacke, finding him a "Most obsequious & insignificant creature", and was concerned about his earlier escapade with the rebels.[24] Finucane, a member of an influential Irish family, made himself answerable for Uniacke's principles and abilities.[25]

The appointment of solicitor general gave Uniacke an entry into Nova Scotian officialdom. Even though he was a law officer of the Crown, he could continue to practise his chosen profession. He had arrived back just before the influx of experienced loyalist lawyers, and he soon had a thriving legal practice that was by 1800 the largest in Nova Scotia.

He needed all the legal work that Halifax, waxing rich on the profits of war, could provide. Creditors of the Uniacke-Delesdernier trading ventures had not forgotten the debts owed them. The largest claim was by John Moyes of the ill-fated *Hopewell* enterprise who, however, was able to obtain only a pittance of the £1000 he claimed he was owed. Uniacke's brother Bartholomew, who had also been disowned by their father, turned up as a disbanded captain of the King's Orange Rangers, and his debts had to be settled. Martha Maria had already borne one son, and to house his growing family he purchased a house on Hollis Street. This was followed by the purchase of a thirty acre farm in the south suburbs. For £1300 he obtained four lots on Argyle Street, the most fashionable street in Halifax, and there in the early 1790's he built one of the finest homes in the city. From 1782 to 1784 he spent over £2,000 on property. As his salary as solicitor general was only £150, his law practice must have been very lucrative indeed. He was truly making his way in the New World.

In these years Nova Scotia was governed by a coterie of Halifax merchants and officials who dominated the council and managed the assembly with a sure instinct for their own survival and aggrandizement. They had brought down one governor who had opposed them and their pecuniary habits, and succeeding governors had little interest

---

24. Hamond to Napean, August 14, 1786, CO 217, Vol. 58, miscellaneous, P.R.O. Hamond, who had been succeeded by John Parr as governor, was in England and defending himself against charges by Parr and Uniacke concerning a dispute over £400.

25. Gibbons commented that Finucane appeared "to be tinctured with national attachments which some Irish recommendations have induced him to procure one Uniacke (who was associated with the rebels in attacking Fort Cumberland) to be appointed solicitor general in my place". Gibbons to J.F.W. Desbarres, January 1, 1782, as quoted in L.G. Power, "Richard John Uniacke", *Collections*, N.S.H.S., Vol. IX, p. 84.

in following suit. Governor John Parr, who arrived in 1782, was soon happily one of them, enjoying his dual salaries as governor and colonel of a regiment. Parr was an Irishman and probably acquainted with the Uniackes. A partnership of mutual interest and affection soon developed between Parr and his solicitor general, with Richard Bulkeley, Chief Justice Bryan Finucane, the merchant brothers of Thomas, James and William Cochran and others, they formed a Halifax Irish connection of considerable influence and power. These sons of Erin founded the Charitable Irish Society in 1786 to provide charity for their needy countrymen, Protestant and Catholic, and a focus for their own social life.[26] Uniacke is given credit for its formation and became its first president. Now well connected and seemingly secure in his adopted land, he thought it only natural to enter into the political life of a colony that was now priding itself on its loyalty to the King and parliament, and whose people expected as a reward the exclusion of New Englanders from the offshore fisheries and the West Indian trade, the sinews of Nova Scotia's commercial life. Uniacke had high expectations and so did his fellow Nova Scotians.

The Fifth Assembly had sat for twelve years and there were many seats vacant, including the one for Sackville township in Cumberland County. Sackville had been the most disaffected township during the rebellion and many of its people had fled, including its assembly member; however, New Englanders still formed the majority. The government in Halifax was determined to restore central control. In 1783 an election was called to fill the vacant Sackville seat with none other than Uniacke, the repentant rebel, as a candidate. Both Uniacke and his Halifax friends may have been somewhat surprised when his candidacy was opposed by a Dr. John Prince. Nothing is known of Prince, but he was probably a newcomer to the district. Thirty-five votes were cast out of an electorate of not more than sixty, and Uniacke was elected with a majority of seventeen.[27]

Ironically, he must have been elected with the support of New Englanders who probably saw in his election one means of regaining the confidence of government. The aftermath of the rebellion was still very much present. Anyone who had been suspected of disloyalty could expect little justice from the local magistrates, as poor Delesdernier discovered when he returned to try and recoup his losses. He found only "prejudice and Malice" prevailing against him; this time, however, it was the military authorities and the Yorkshiremen who

---

26. Records of the Charitable Irish Society, MG 20, Vol. 65, P.A.N.S.
27. Return of Sackville Township election, 1783. RG 1, Vol. 409, No. 12, P.A.N.S.

harassed him, rather than the New Englanders.[28] An officer of the garrison forcibly seized a room in Delesdernier's house for a recently arrived loyalist. The magistrates, all Yorkshiremen, refused to assist Delesdernier to obtain justice, but the New Englanders rallied to the unfortunate soul and complained to the judges of the Supreme Court about the improper use of military power. Uniacke took up the case and Parr administered a stern rebuke to the offending magistrates.

In 1783 Uniacke was thirty and could look to the future with confidence, for fortune was smiling on him and his intelligence and energy marked him out for the promised promotion to attorney general. Very much the confidant of the governor, he was already the recipient of his patronage, and although not yet wealthy, he had every expectation of becoming so. Thus his future seemed secure in that year before the main rush of loyalists arrived.

The patrician and acerbic loyalist Edward Winslow, who spent the winter of 1783-4 in Halifax, early took note of Uniacke, chastising him as "a great lubbery insolent Irish rebel".[29] When Uniacke among others protested the partition of Nova Scotia to provide a loyalist haven in the new colony of New Brunswick, Winslow lost no time in characterizing the signers of the remonstrance as "a class of gentry not remarkable for their loyalty, viz. Uniacke".[30]

Uniacke's election with the support of the New Englanders must have incensed those who had been loyal in 1776; no doubt they were amused when, in 1784, after the partition of the province, Sackville became part of the new colony of New Brunswick and Uniacke's constituency disappeared. Uniacke now had to fight for his political and financial survival against the hated Americans. He triumphed, but only just.

---

28. Delesdernier to Sir Frederick Haldimand, October 30, 1778, transcript. RG 1, Vol. 367, No. 14, P.A.N.S.

29. Edward Winslow to Ward Chipman, July 7, 1783, *Winslow Papers, A.D. 1776-1826*, ed., Rev. W.O. Raymond (St. John, N.B., 1901) p. 97. He called Gibbons "an ignorant harmless nincompoop".

30. Edward Winslow to George Leonard, October 5, 1784, *Ibid.*, p. 240.

Chapter Two

A Great Lubbery Insolent Irish Rebel

The migration of the loyalists in 1783 was the largest, most complex and difficult migration of people in colonial experience. Nearly twenty thousand people came to Nova Scotia; they doubled the population to over 40,000, opened up new areas to settlement, and accelerated its political, economic and cultural development.

Most of the loyalists came from the middle and southern colonies, a cross-section of American colonial life with a mixture of town and country, Anglicans and Dissenters, and English, Irish and Scots. There was also a patrician group who settled mainly in Halifax. They were men of ability; law was their profession, and it was their ambition to retrieve what they had lost through their loyalty to the Crown.

A fierce struggle ensued between Uniacke and this group that lasted until his appointment as attorney general in 1797. These loyalists readily accepted Edward Winslow's characterization that Uniacke was a "great lubbery insolent Irish rebel". It was an affront to their loyalty, to their whole melancholy migration, that a former rebel should hold an office that they believed should be theirs by right of their allegiance to king and parliament. Nonetheless, the characterization was unjust; Uniacke did what he could to relieve the distress of the refugees. Most Nova Scotians greeted their arrival with indifference.

Uniacke had his faults, but lack of compassion was not one of them. The patrician lawyers, however, were determined that he should never become attorney general. They initiated the quarrel and gave him no choice but to fight back with all the skill and influence he could command. When he became convinced that the newcomers, as the loyalists were called, were "endeavouring to establish a superiority over the old inhabitants",[1] he assumed the leadership in the assembly of the pre-loyalists, or oldcomers.

---

1. Uniacke to Frederick Robinson, President of the Board of Trade, November 16, 1822, Board of Trade, 6/253, p. 34, P.R.O. He also told Robinson he had used every exertion "to prevent the Government from taking any part with either side, and by such means notwithstanding the violent lengths to which party was carried, the Government was respected by both sides...", p. 35.

The transportation of the loyalists was organised as far as was possible by the British Army in New York. The government in Halifax was ill-prepared to receive the thousands of men, women and children, and the burden of meeting their needs fell on a few officials with very limited resources. Establishing the loyalists on their lands entailed the issuing of over six thousand grants of land. When the attorney general, Richard Gibbons, refused to accept reduced fees for granting lands, Uniacke as solicitor general assumed the responsibility for escheating 1.3 million acres and assisting in the preparation of the grants.[2] In the assembly he drafted legislation to relieve the distress of those refugees who were completely destitute and for the creation of the new county of Shelburne, where 10,000 loyalists had arrived dreaming of a new Philadelphia or Boston.

In 1784, when Gibbons was promoted to be chief justice of Cape Breton, the attorney generalship again became vacant. Uniacke's claims to succeed were strong. There was however another claimant, Samuel Sampson Blowers, a former solicitor general of New York and a staunch loyalist. Ten years Uniacke's senior and a graduate of Harvard, Blowers had already been offered the attorney generalship of New Brunswick, but had refused the appointment. His loyalty, seniority and experience made him the principal claimant and he was duly appointed. Circumstances made Uniacke and Blowers rivals; marked differences in character did much to make them enemies. A short, thin man of untiring energy, Blowers could never forget his experiences during the American War and looked upon Nova Scotia as a haven from the turmoil he had witnessed. He had none of Uniacke's wit, lust for life or imagination. Although he gained much respect for his professional competence, he never displayed Uniacke's style as a leader and seems to have resented his rival's influence with Nova Scotians.

Blower's appointment was not a surprise. Perhaps as a palliative, Parr preceeded it by making Uniacke advocate general of the Vice Admiralty Court, an office which would be instrumental in the making of his fortune. The laws of trade and navigation came under the jurisdiction of this court, and in war it became the court of adjudication for captured prize ships. The fees for court officials were lucrative and were the basis of many fortunes before the Napoleonic War ended. Blowers, who had made substantial sums when judge of the Vice Admiralty Court in New York in the last year of the American

2. Memorial of Uniacke to Portland, c. 1800, CO217, Vol. 74, miscellaneous, P.R.O. He had been requesting payment for some years and claimed he had had great difficulty in doing the job because of the opposition of the original grantees.

Rebellion, challenged Uniacke's appointment, claiming it should come with that of attorney general.

As a result of a dispute in 1786 over whether two American ships had discharged their cargoes legally in Halifax, Blowers and Uniacke took their quarrel to Britain. Blowers and another loyalist lawyer, Jonathan Sterns, acting for the owners, had secured permission from the Vice Admiralty Court to unload the cargoes. This had been done without Uniacke's knowledge as advocate general, and he was enraged at what he perceived as an attempt to outwit and supplant him. The dispute went to Govenor Parr and to London to the Secretary of State for the Colonies. In his memorial Blowers argued that Uniacke should never have received the office of advocate general which, by custom, should have come to him as attorney general, and charged that no one "ever has been or will be found more deficient of loyalty" than Uniacke.[3] Not to be outdone, Uniacke imputed support of smuggling to Blowers and Sterns, informing the secretary of state that "the sagacity of these people [Americans] and the powerful friends they have made in this Government" had defeated all Parr's attempts to stop illegal trading with the United States.[4] The British government refused to concern itself with this colonial squabble and left it to Parr to sort out. There was never any doubt that Uniacke would retain the office, but there is evidence that an arrangment was reached which gave Blowers a right to some of the court fees.

The loyalists despised Governor Parr and his officials; by the rules of their time, they would hold office until old age or death parted them from it. Ambitious and impatient, the loyalists saw little hope of obtaining any office, particularly while Parr was governor. Hence it was natural that they should turn to the assembly as a forum where they could vent their frustrations and challenge the pre-loyalist office-holders. The Tories of the American Revolution rapidly became the Whigs of Nova Scotia, using the Sixth Assembly (1785-1792) to challenge the old order.

It was a reforming assembly characterized by much-needed measures of political, economic and educational improvement. The loyalists had only thirteen members out of a house of thirty-nine, but their abilities and energy soon gave them dominance.[5] With

---

3. Blowers to Nepean, January 10, 1786, CO217, Vol. 58, miscellaneous, P.R.O. A memorial by Blowers in which he enclosed one by Uniacke and replied to changes contained in Uniacke's.
4. Ibid, Uniacke to Nepean, January 27, 1786.
5. For the loyalists in the Sixth Assembly see M.G. Morison, "The Evolution of Political Parties in Nova Scotia, 1758-1848" (unpublished M.A. thesis, Dalhousie University, 1949) pp. 17-27.

considerable skill they gained the support of the members from outside of Halifax, and broke the hold of the Halifax establishment over the proceedings of the assembly. The loyalists did not try to form a party; on the contrary, there was no vote in the seven sessions clearly dividing loyalist and pre-loyalist. There were also divisions among the loyalists themselves and their inferior numbers meant that, had they worked as a party, defeat would certainly have been their lot. Nonetheless, there was an undercurrent of tension between loyalist and pre-loyalist members, the latter suspecting, with some justification, that self-interest rather than a desire for reform motivated the loyalists.

Under Uniacke's leadership the last two sessions of the Fifth Assembly had begun the process of reforming the archaic rules for conducting house business. As well as being solicitor general, and the most important office-holder in the assembly, he was elected clerk of the house in 1783. Virtually single-handedly he had managed the proceedings, drafting addresses and bills as required, and acting as liason between the assembly and the council. He had also used his position as *de facto* house leader to introduce rules and procedures to conform to those of the British House of Commons. His initiatives raised the prestige of the assembly and given its members greater confidence in their dealings with the appointed council. But the predominant role Uniacke played in the Fifth Assembly could not continue into the Sixth.

In the 1785 election he ran for one of the four Halifax County seats and was elected, along with another oldcomer and two loyalists. The assembly elected Blowers as speaker and then became embroiled in an intra-loyalist dispute over the election of one Joseph Brewer for Shelburne township. Brewer was opposed by Isaac Wilkins, whose cause was taken up by Blowers. It was natural that Blowers should do so, as Wilkins, a former member of the New York assembly and noted for his toryism, was of Blowers' class of patrician loyalist. Brewer's supporters, interestingly, did not seek the support of another loyalist member, but approached Uniacke; it is probable that Uniacke had been one of the officials in Halifax who had blocked earlier attempts by Wilkins and some other loyalists to gain large grants of land at the expense of their fellow loyalists. This and his other efforts on their behalf was sufficient reason for the Brewer supporters to turn to him. He took up the case, but after considerable debate the assembly decided for Wilkins.

In Shelburne the dispute continued to simmer. Two months later, an address to Uniacke appeared in *The Nova Scotia Gazette,* thanking him for his "true Spirit of Patriotism".[6] In his reply he eulogized the Shelburne loyalists "who have been so eminently distinguished for their Loyalty".[7] The address to Uniacke angered Wilkins' supporters, but they were wary of creating too much party feeling. Their strategy, as outlined by James Clark to his fellow Shelburne loyalist, Gideon White, was for the "real loyalists" as they called themselves, to give "every attention and mark of respect" to Blowers while "for political reasons... not [to] be pointed towards Uniacke nor discover anything that had the appearance of faction or party".[8] Gideon White, a Massachusetts loyalist and a prominent supporter of Wilkins, held no personal animosity towards Uniacke and often used his legal services.

The 1786 session passed with only one row between Uniacke and the loyalists. It involved a letter by Thomas Barclay to some members of the assembly disputing a committee report that set aside the election of a loyalist friend in Annapolis County. Barclay, a lawyer and former officer in the Loyal American Regiment, was a brilliant and eloquent debater, but his resentment at not receiving an office marked his every action. His letter gave much offence, and his fellow loyalist Isaac Wilkins, realizing that Barclay did not have the majority with him, moved that the letter be simply dismissed. However, upon the urgings of Uniacke, the assembly defeated Wilkins' motion, and then passed one of Uniacke's demanding a formal apology. Barclay, accepting his defeat, made the required apology; however, he did not forget Uniacke's adding of a touch of salt to the wound. This "Speechifying and Cabaling" amused oldcomer George Monk, although he hoped for a total rejection of the two parties because of the feelings being aroused throughout the province by the clashes between old-and newcomers.[9] The political posturing of Uniacke and Barclay was watched with some interest outside the walls of the assembly.

There now erupted a controversy over the conduct of the judges of the Supreme Court that pitted newcomer against oldcomer and loyalist against loyalist, and developed into a major challenge to Governor Parr and his council.[10] Chief Justice Bryan Finucane had died in 1785 and the two assistant judges, Isaac Deschamps and James Brenton, had been carrying the full burden. Deschamps had no legal training other

6. *The Nova-Scotia Gazette and The Weekly Chronicle*, February 21, 1786.

7. *Ibid*, For further letters on the dispute see *ibid*, March 28, 1786 and April 18, 1786.

8. Jas. Clarke to Gideon White, March 9, 1786, MG 1, Vol. 949, No. 404, P.A.N.S.

9. George Monk to John Wentworth, June 9, 1786, MG 1, Vol. 970, pp. 77-78, P.A.N.S.

10. See Margaret Ells, "Nova Scotian Sparks of Liberty", *Dalhousie Review*, Vol. XVI, No. 4 (January 1937) pp. 473-492 for a detailed examination of the dispute.

than what he had picked up as a judge of the Inferior Court of Common Pleas for Kings County. Brenton had been junior member of the Rhode Island bar before coming to Nova Scotia, and had been promoted to the bench for want of anyone better.

Near the end of the 1787 session, the assembly went into secret session to consider the public dissatisfaction with the administration of justice. Both Uniacke and Barclay gave evidence of their dissatisfaction. Uniacke as solicitor general had every reason to be circumspect in his criticism, but he was critical enough to give the impression he supported some reform.[11] He did not seem to have realized that the loyalists were aiming at the removal of the judges and securing the appointments for themselves.

In private conversation Blowers had said he would use his influence with Governor General Lord Dorchester to have the judges removed, but during the secret session he sat in "solemn silence".[12] He was greatly alarmed by rumours that Parr had recommended Uniacke to be chief justice, and by his silence he hoped to influence Parr to have himself appointed.[13] His reward soon came: promotion to the council, the first "real loyalist" to be appointed.

Uniacke now realized that it was important for him to support Parr and his council in the face of the challenge of the loyalist-led faction. The Halifax by-election in 1788 pitted Charles Morris, a supporter of the council and the judges, against Jonathan Sterns, the loyalist attorney, who had bitterly denounced the conduct of the judges. In a highly spirited election in which many were wounded and one person killed, Morris triumphed, and he was carried through the streets of Halifax. The Morris and Sterns factions continued the battle in the streets for another three days, and eventually the troops of the garrison had to intervene to stop the rioting.[14]

Uniacke saw this election as a challenge to Parr's government, and

---

11. A pamphlet was published entitled *Extracts from the proceedings of His Majesty's Council February 21 & 28, 1788, in reference to complaints of improper and irregular administration of justice in the Supreme Court of Nova Scotia* (Halifax 1788). The pamphlet is almost entirely of letters republished from newspapers no longer extant and is the principal source for the judges' affair in 1787 and 1788.
12. *Ibid*, Letter of Jonathan Sterns to S.S. Blowers, *Halifax Journal*, March 19, 1788.
13. Jonathan Bliss to S.S. Blowers, May 20, 1787, MG 1, Vol. 1603, P.A.N.S. In fact one of the Loyalist Claims Commissioners, Jeremy Pemberton, was appointed but he never presided and resigned soon after he was appointed.
14. *The Nova Scotia Gazette and Weekly Chronicle*, February 26, 1788. It has generally been assumed that it was Charles Morris II who was elected, but it appears reasonably certain that it was his son. The winner was carried on the shoulders of his fellow citizens to "his father's house". Charles Morris I had been dead for seven years and so it must have been Charles Morris III who was carried to his father's (Charles Morris II) house.

tied by interest and friendship to the Morris faction he came out in its support. The loyalists saw his act as a "defection" from their side to that of the Council.[15] This violent by-election of 1788 gave birth to Uniacke's antipathy to faction.

As soon as Blowers' promotion to the council was known, both Uniacke and Barclay began canvassing for support to succeed him as speaker.[16] The oldcomers rallied to Uniacke and he defeated Barclay.

Dissatisfied with replies of Governor Parr and the council, the assembly in 1790 began impeachment proceedings against the judges, with Barclay as prosecuting attorney. Uniacke laid down how the proceedings would be conducted, prefacing his remarks with a statement that showed he was under considerable pressure. He admitted that although he had formerly been critical of the judges, he was now clearly opposed to any further proceedings against them.[17] The assembly, stirred up by the denunciations of the conduct of the judges and the council by Barclay and Wilkins, was in no mood for any accommodation over the judges. They were duly impeached for "High Crimes and Misdemeanours", and the assembly requested the King that they be given a regular trial. Not content with simply having the proceedings sent to London, the assembly, upon the urgings of Barclay, passed a resolution to provide £200 to employ an agent in London to argue its case. During this debate Uniacke made clear "his general disapprobation of the proceedings against the judges",[18] although he somewhat qualified it by supporting the resolution on the agent. The hearings before the Privy Council Committee did not take place until 1792 and the verdict was favourable to the judges, who retained their posts. However, by then the British goverment had accepted that the appointment of a competent chief justice from outside the colony was a necessity. They sent out Thomas Strange from England to fill the position.

During the impeachment proceedings, Uniacke seems to have controlled his temper; however, during the debate on the fees levied on coastal shipping by the naval officer, Winkworth Tonge, he threw caution aside. The assembly in its 1790 session conducted an investigation into the fee schedule, and neither Blowers nor Uniacke was able to find any act requiring vessels to enter or clear at the naval

---

15. Joseph Alpin to Jonathan Sterns, May 5, 1788, MG 1, Vol. 793, No. 3, P.A.N.S.
16. D.C. Harvey, ed., *The Diary of Simeon Perkins, 1780-1789*, (Champlain Society, Toronto, 1958) February 9, 1788, p. 412 and April 3, 1790, p. 302.
17. Proceedings of the House of Assembly, *The Nova-Scotia Magazine*, April, 1790, p. 302.
18. *The Weekly Chronicle*, June 25, 1791.

offices in the various ports. Uniacke then drew up a declamatory bill to reflect this legal opinion; however, the assembly reached a compromise over the fees with Tonge, and the bill was never passed.

It was the outlying townships which most felt the burden of the fees, and Uniacke maintained a close relationship with the townships through his legal practice and his association with the merchant community. He would not have been elected speaker without the support of their members, and his own antipathy to regulations and fees that inhibited colonial trading placed him on the side of men like Simeon Perkins, the Liverpool diarist and merchant, who opposed the fees. He intervened in the debate from the chair, and, according to Tonge, "advancing such falsehoods with that confidence which generally accompanies truth and a degree of effrontery which no other person can equal".[19] The last phrase catches an aspect of Uniacke's character that was occasionally to get him into unnecessary trouble. Caught up in the heat of debate, his undoubted eloquence could be marred by personal attacks such as those against the elderly and ill Tonge. He always deeply regretted these outbursts and in this instance published an apology.

The procedures for raising and appropriating funds in Nova Scotia were not those of the British parliament, but based upon informal agreements between the council and the assembly. Until 1786, Nova Scotia followed the "loose and irregular" practice (as Uniacke called it) of having no appropriations act. After this, on the instructions of the British government, the procedure was for the governor, with advice of his council, to prepare estimates and to present these to the assembly, which incorporated them with the money resolutions of individual members into an appropriations bill. This bill was then sent for concurrence to the council, which, when the assembly was in session, acted as the upper house of the legislature. Taxes were raised by revenue bills that originated in the assembly and were also sent to the council for agreement. The constitutional issue that now arose was whether the council had the right to amend money bills already passed by the assembly. It was generally accepted that the council had the constitutional right to reject a money bill completely. However rejection of the appropriations bill meant the executive had no authority to expend any funds in the coming year, and if the revenue bills were rejected, no taxes could be collected.

The council, much embittered by the judges dispute and alarmed by the rising provincial debt, began in the 1789 session to assert its

---

19. *The Royal Gazette and the Nova Scotia Advertiser*, May 11, 1790.

claim to amend money bills. The ensuing dispute reached an impasse in the 1791 session when Parr was forced to dissolve the assembly without an appropriations bill having been passed. A much-chastened council in the next session bowed to the will of the assembly and passed the appropriations bill.

In 1784 Uniacke had led the assembly in rejecting the council's claim to amend money bills.[20] He had done so upon British parliamentary precedent, the House of Lords having long conceded that claim to the House of Commons. However, it was also a rule that members could not originate money resolutions, whereas the Nova Scotian assembly followed American colonial practice of members initiating such resolutions without the sanction of the executive. To have conceded the council's claim to amend money bills would have given that appointed body such power that the balance between the executive and legislative branches would have shifted dramatically to the former. To the individual assemblyman, his claim to his constitutents' share of the public purse was his main *raison d'etre*. This, however, resulted in a haphazard and inefficient expenditure of the revenue, and over which the executive could exercise little control. Governors who wanted to initiate major improvements would often find their designs thwarted by the assembly, which placed local concerns first. Until responsible government and the party system, the executive remained weak; to gain its ends it had to rely upon the use of patronage. The demand for offices and the prerogative of the executive to dispense them did much to make colonial government work in Nova Scotia as well as it did.

No one understood with greater clarity than Uniacke the weaknesses of colonial government. Throughout his long public life he strove to have the Nova Scotian constitution modelled upon that of the British, with the aim of strengthening the executive. The solution he proposed in 1791 to solve the appropriations dispute was to adopt as much of the British parliamentary practice as possible.[21] He wanted the rule accepted whereby no request for money made by an assemblyman could be included in the appropriations bill unless it had been first recommended by the governor. By this procedure he hoped to insure greater executive control over expenditures while not infringing upon the undoubted right of the assembly to originate all money bills.

Uniacke put his proposal to Chief Justice Strange, who was president of the council when it sat in its legislative role. Strange turned

---

20. *Journals of the Legislative Assembly* (hereafter *J.L.A.*) December 3, 1784.
21. Opinion of the Attorney General, enclosure No. 2 in Croke to Castlereagh, April 3, 1809, CO217, Vol. 85, P.R.O.

it down, giving as his main reason that, while in the British parliament some of the King's ministers sat in the commons and could readily signify approval or disapproval of money requests, in Nova Scotia no members of the council sat in the assembly. There was no constitutional reason why they could not. Later Uniacke advocated that some members of the council be drawn from the assembly, but in 1791 he was most concerned to find a solution to reconcile the competing constitutional claims of the council and the assembly. A variation of his proposal was accepted whereby the assembly sent each money resolution separately to the council, and if there was disagreement, it was sorted out in conference between committees of each branch. The agreed resolutions were then put into the appropriations bill and passed by both houses.

The feuding between the assembly and the council made Uniacke's speakership an onerous and difficult task. Since there was no formal party structure, it was the speaker who was expected to provide leadership as the first commoner. It was not unusual for him to intervene in debates and to draft legislation. A strong speaker, and Uniacke was certainly that, exercised far more influence and authority than his nominal role of maintaining order suggested. As first commoner Uniacke was sworn to uphold the rights of the assembly and if he had failed to do so, his speakership would have been challenged. There is no evidence that his position was ever challenged in the acrimonious debates of this period. His firmness and "racy humour"[22] did much to preserve order in at times a very unruly house. Barclay, whom he had defeated for the speakership, never seems to have lost an opportunity to vent his scarcasm, and on one occasion when he suggested Uniacke was not well acquainted with the wishes of his constitutents, Uniacke rose from his speaker's chair and delivered a stern rebuke to Barclay, who immediately apologized.[23]

From the spring of 1791 Uniacke's political influence went into eclipse and was not restored before the end of the decade. The causes were partly of his own making but primarily a consequence of the appointment of John Wentworth as governor upon the death of Parr in November 1791. It was clear that the pre-loyalist Halifax establishment would soon be supplanted by Wentworth appointees. With the death of Parr and the retirement of Richard Bulkeley as provincial secretary, the Irish connection that had so benefitted Uniacke in the previous decade lost its influence. The fall of the old Halifax order was sealed in the 1793

22. Beamish Murdoch, *History of Nova Scotia*, Vol. III, (Halifax, 1867) p. 98.
23. Proceedings of the House of Assembly, *The Nova-Scotia Magazine*, March 1790, p. 218.

elections when Uniacke, Charles Morris and Charles Hill stepped aside and their seats were taken by loyalists Jonathan Sterns, Michael Wallace and Lawrence Hartshorne. In some bitterness Uniacke had declared before the election that "he should not come into the House again".[24] He, as well as anyone, could see the consequences for himself of Wentworth's appointment.

Uniacke made no attempt to ingratiate himself with the new order, and even antagonized Chief Justice Strange, who had been sent out to report on the Nova Scotian bar as well as to be chief justice. Strange was a young Englishman with a reputation as an excellent theoretical lawyer, but he had had little court room experience and he was somewhat unsure of himself. In a case involving debts, Uniacke conducted his summing up in a manner that Strange considered "a personal challenge" to his ability to preside as chief justice. Uniacke had begun his summing up by intimating that he would take four or five hours and go through nine statutes and seventy-two cases. Much to the amusement of the spectators who crowded into the court room, he opened three large bags of legal books and with much pretentiousness placed them in rows on a table in front of him. Strange chastized Uniacke for "slovenly and unlawyerlike" behaviour. An argument ensued in which Uniacke displayed "improper boldness".[25]

It is likely that under the assistant judges and even under Chief Justice Finucane Uniacke had been allowed great leniency in conducting his cases. Dressed in legal black, wearing a full bottom wig and using his gigantic stature, which was matched by a "voice of thunder", he could dominate a court room with impressive ease.[26] Always eloquent, he could alternate between wit and solemnity with theatrical skill. Strange was not prepared to concede Uniacke the leniency he had had in the past and was determined to establish his authority. Uniacke had no choice but to submit; however, he does not seem to have done so with particularly good grace.

As so often in these colonial contretemps, both parties submitted memorials to the governor and Strange in some agitation reported his side to London. No further action was taken. However, Uniacke must have damaged his reputation at the Colonial Office and had certainly gained the antipathy of Strange, who, in the following year in his report

---

24. Strange to Cumberland (provincial agent) April 28, 1793, CO217, Vol. 64, miscellaneous, P.R.O.

25. Strange to Scrope Bernard (undersecretary of state) Secret, April 2, 1791, CO217, Vol. 63, miscellaneous, P.R.O.

26. From a lecture by the Rev. J.C. Cochran, Vertical Manuscript File: Cochran, Rev. J.C. Lectures, P.A.N.S.

on the Nova Scotian bar, refused to recommend Uniacke as "a fit person to supply a vacancy upon the Bench".[27] He recommended that Blowers should succeed him as chief justice and Jonathan Sterns as attorney general when vacancies should occur.

The enmity between Blowers and Uniacke had become so deep that in the autumn of 1791, Blowers challenged Uniacke to a duel. Apparently Uniacke had dismissed a negro servant whom Blowers had then taken into service. This so angered Uniacke that he said some "rude things" to Blowers, who immediately challenged. Strange intervened to prevent a duel between the two law officers of the Crown by binding them over for £1000 to keep the peace. Oldcomer and newcomer friction was very much present, the sureties for Uniacke being prominent pre-loyalists and those for Blowers equally prominent loyalists. According to Barclay, a not-impartial witness, Blowers told Uniacke that he was prepared to break the bond; this so "frightened Uniacke that he begged pardon", and the "Honor of Massachusetts . . . [came] off with flying colours".[28] It is highly doubtful that Uniacke begged pardon, but he may well have apologized, as it was he who had apparently offered the insult and initiated the foolish quarrel.

Duelling was illegal, although occasionally happening in the garrison, and neither Uniacke nor Blowers had ever demonstrated any martial spirit. Blowers had fled to England at the beginning of the American Revolution and only returned when he thought the British were winning. During the Cumberland Rebellion Uniacke had shown few soldierly virtues. It was probably concern for his family that caused him to refuse Blowers' second challenge. Clearly, however, their antipathy towards each other was far deeper than the existing evidence would suggest. It certainly must have been a contributing cause to Uniacke's withdrawal from public life.

By the time the new loyalist governor John Wentworth stepped ashore in May 1792, Uniacke had been driven from public life. His enemies had temporarily triumphed. His pride precluded any attempt at a reconciliation with the new order. He was not a beaten man; however, he was a very angry and embittered one and as determined as ever not to be denied the attorney generalship when it next became vacant.

---

27. A memorandum by Strange prepared on the direction of Secretary of State Dundas, March 10, 1792, CO217, Vol. 63, miscellaneous, P.R.O.
28. Thomas Barclay to Rufus Chandler, Annapolis, November 6, 1791, as quoted in George L. Rives, ed., *Selections from the Correspondence of Thomas Barclay* (Harper Brothers, New York, 1894) p. 35. In the Nova Scotia Supreme Court records there is a note dated October 4, 1791 binding Uniacke and Blowers to keep the peace, RG 39, Series C, Vol. 79, 1798, P.A.N.S.

Chapter Three

Secretly Connected with Seditious Purposes

John Wentworth was fifty-five when he was appointed governor of Nova Scotia. Born into a prominent New England family, he was marked for high office and wealth.[1] Educated at Harvard, where he became a lifelong friend of a future president of the United States, John Adams, he succeeded his uncle as governor of New Hampshire in 1767 at the age of thirty-one. Five years earlier he had married his cousin, Frances Wentworth, one of the most beautiful and self-willed women in New England.

A man of great physical endurance, fair learning and extravagant tastes, Wentworth was swept aside by the American Revolution, having to leave his governor's mansion in the night with his wife and infant son and flee to the protection of the British lines. In 1778 he went to England; in 1783 he came to Nova Scotia with a commission as Surveyor General of the King's Woods and a salary of £700. This was not much compared to the royal governorship of New Hampshire, but much better than the lot of many of his fellow loyalists, who had to survive a winter in tents on the slopes of Citadel Hill and in Point Pleasant Park. They still referred to him as "His Excellency",[2] and it was well understood that if any loyalist succeeded to the governorship upon Parr's departure or demise, it would be John Wentworth.

In 1789 Wentworth went to England once more to employ what influence he could in his search for promotion, and probably hoping

---

1. For biographies of Wentworth see L.S. Mayo, *John Wentworth: Governor of New Hampshire, 1767-1775* (Harvard, 1921) and Sir Adams Archibald, "Life of Sir John Wentworth: Governor of Nova Scotia", 1792-1808, *Collections*, N.S.H.S., Vol. XX, pp. 43-109.

2. See for example Thomas Barclay to Governor Wentworth, November 27, 1785, MG 1, Vol. 939, No. 21, P.A.N.S. Barclay remarks he was prepared to accept any office but had little hopes of receiving one at the hands of Parr because the pre-loyalist office-holders were doing everything in their power to dissuade Parr from "conferring offices on us unfortunate Loyalists".

also to gratify the insatiable desires of his society-conscious wife, whose promiscuity had become the talk of Halifax. The Marquis of Rockingham, who had been leader of the Whig faction bearing his name, had died in 1782, but his faction lived on under the leadership of the Duke of Portland and Henry Dundas, eloquently supported by the rhetoric of Edmund Burke. A childless couple, the Rockinghams were godparents to the Wentworths' only child; upon the Marquis' death the estate had passed to his nephew, Earl Fitzwilliam, and to him and to Rockingham's widow the Wentworths turned for support. Wentworth was so desperate for office that he had been prepared to accept the governorship of Cape Breton; however, he and Frances were saved from that disagreeable alternative. John King, the permanent undersecretary at the Colonial Office, was a personal friend, and once Parr's death in November 1791 became known, a concerted effort was mounted on both sides of the Atlantic to have Wentworth succeed Parr.[3] The appointment was in the gift of Dundas, the Secretary of State for War and the Colonies, and in regard for the memory of Lord Rockingham he bestowed it on Wentworth.

In the first decade of his governorship he was energetic in his pursuit of measures to re-establish the provincial credit, assist agriculture, commerce and the fisheries, and construct public works. Within a short time he succeeded in providing leadership to a society that was at last beginning to show confidence in its destiny. The staunch loyalists called him the "Father of the Province", forgetting that there was a Nova Scotia before their arrival.[4]

He entertained lavishly, drawing into his circle society-conscious Haligonians and officers of the garrison. In one eleven month period 2,437 people dined at Government House.[5] Numbers there were, but Frances kept a close eye on the invitation list and anyone in the least disfavour with her husband was ruthlessly excluded. In Wentworth's Nova Scotia political disfavour meant social ostracization.

---

3. See Lady Rockingham's correspondence concerning Governor Wentworth's appointment 1791-2, original documents from Wharcliffe Muniments, property of the Earl of Wharcliffe, microfilm, biography, Francis Wentworth, P.A.N.S.

4. Lady Wentworth to Lady Rockingham, November 19, 1801, MG 1, Vol. 941, No. 4, P.A.N.S. (Wentworth was made a baronet in 1795).

5. For the story of Government House and its furnishings see J.S. Martell, "Government House", *Bulletin of the Public Archives of Nova Scotia*, Vol. 1, No. 4, 1939, and by the same author *The Romance of Government House*, (King's Printer, Halifax, 1939).

Wentworth came to his governorship determined to uphold the royal prerogative and to tolerate no democratic or republican tendencies. For him, personal loyalty to himself was synonomous with loyalty to the Crown. As Uniacke and William Cottnam Tonge discovered, to cross Wentworth resulted in being charged with disloyalty. Those who did not cross him were rewarded with appointments, contacts and favours. Wentworth wove a web of patronage that not only tied almost everyone of any influence to him personally and to the cause of government, but also did much to reconcile old-and newcomers.[6] There was some truth in Frances Wentworth's comment to Lady Rockingham that "strangers observe... that they never were before in any country where one party made the whole society..."[7]

Wentworth lost no time in castigating Uniacke as disloyal and accusing him of seditious behaviour during the threatened French attack in the summer of 1793. Nova Scotians had learned of war with France in April of that year. Halifax was garrisoned by very weak forces and measures were taken to put the militia into a state of readiness. Two battalions of militia were enrolled in Halifax and Uniacke became second-in-command of the Second Battalion. The *Portland* Packet arrived from New York on July 23rd with the alarming news of the arrival of a French fleet there, presumably preparing to attack Halifax. That evening a town meeting was held and a committee, which included Uniacke, was selected to present an address to Wentworth.[8] This address, which Wentworth sent to Henry Dundas, was blunt about the defenceless state of Halifax. There was fear that the large quantity of military stores and commercial goods in Halifax would tempt the French fleet to attack. The commercial goods were of great concern to those London Merchants Trading to Halifax who had shipped them on credit. Having obtained details of the vulnerability of Halifax from their colleagues, these merchants warned Dundas to expect trouble in parliament. On January 29th, 1794 the Irishman Richard Brinsley Sheridan, the famous playwright and a fierce critic of

---

6. See Margaret Ells, "Governor Wentworth's Patronage", *Collections, N.S.H.S.*, Vol. XXV, pp. 49-73.

7. Lady Wentworth to Lady Rockingham, November 19, 1801, MG 1, Vol. 941, No. 4, P.A.N.S.

8. *The Royal Gazette and The Nova Scotia Advertiser.* July 23, 1793. The address was signed by Uniacke and nine others.

the war, rose in the House of Commons and read a letter from Halifax describing the wretched state of its defences.[9]

This letter, which Sheridan said came from an unnamed merchant, was dated December 7th. On that same date Wentworth had written his friend John King at the Colonial Office that he feared "our Solicitor General is not perfectly right — He cannot escape my vigilance, if I find him certainly unworthy, he must be superseded".[10] Wentworth clearly believed that Uniacke was engaging in or instigating what Wentworth chose to interpret as seditious activities. It is quite possible that Uniacke was one of Sheridan's correspondents, as Sheridan later claimed he had received upwards of fifty letters from Halifax, including some from government officials. Sheridan continued his attacks on Dundas, who, in reply, tabled Wentworth's glowing reports of his own efforts to place Halifax in a state of defence. In turn Sheridan charged that the reports were grossly deceiving and that Wentworth was more interested in the emoluments from the regiment he was raising, the Royal Nova Scotia Regiment, which he officered and his friends.

Calm returned to Halifax when word was received that the French fleet had sailed for France in April 1794. Wentworth blamed Uniacke for the "popular inquietudes on Mr. Sheridan's speech and the letters to him" and was determined that Uniacke should not be promoted.[11] As he told King, Uniacke's "conduct is dark and insidious secretly connected with seditious purposes, & giving advice against the service". He was not ready as yet to dismiss him but King should refer to him any attempts by the Uniacke family and the Irish peer, Baron George Beresford, to use influence for Uniacke's promotion.

There is no direct evidence that Uniacke was involved in the correspondence to Sheridan but it is more than likely that he was. Uniacke was undoubtedly soliciting support from the Irish patrons of his family for the day when vacancies would occur in the Nova Scotian government.

---

9. Speeches, January 29, 1794, "Naval Power for 1794", p. 281 and also one on February 21, 1794, "Defensive State of Halifax", pp. 287-8 in *The Speeches of the Right Honourable Richard Brinsley Sheridan*, edited by A Constitutional Friend., Vol. III, 1842. See also a letter to Dundas from a friend, August 31, 1793, warning that the opposition in parliament would be given "a handle" if the stores were destroyed, CO 217, Vol. 64, miscellaneous, and letter from London Merchants Trading to Halifax to Dundas, February 19, 1794, CO 217, Vol. 65, miscellaneous, P.R.O. There was such fear in Halifax that on one occasion when the alarm was given, falsely as it turned out, the inhabitants, including Wentworth, packed their belongings and headed outside the city.

10. Wentworth to King, private, December 7, 1793, CO 217, Vol. 36, P.R.O.

11. Wentworth to King, private and secret. January 23, 1795, CO 217, Vol. 36, P.R.O.

The arrival in 1794 of Edward, Duke of Kent, the fourth son of George III, as commander of the troops in Nova Scotia and New Brunswick, gave to Halifax society a sense of the *beau monde* that was long remembered. The future father of Queen Victoria, with his mistress Julie St. Laurent, entertained and was entertained with such lavishness that the six years of his stay became known as the "golden age" of Nova Scotia. In the 1790's Halifax was a bleak garrison town with no public buildings, other than Saint Paul's, of any architectural merit. By 1820 it had an array of graceful Georgian edifices unmatched in British North America. These provided an architectural relief to an increasingly sophisticated and prosperous society. To Prince Edward, an amateur architect himself, must go much of the credit for inspiring this change.

A martinet with a strong sense of decorum and propriety, he soon imposed a high moral tone on a garrison and a society where gambling and drunkeness had been only too common. He was careful always to bestow his favour impartially, and even in the last years of his unhappy life he did what he could for Nova Scotians who solicited his favour. Uniacke, although excluded from Frances Wentworth's table, was not so from the Duke's, and as a token of his regard for Uniacke the Duke gave him two Louis XVI chairs, one of which is on display today in the drawing room of Mount Uniacke. Upon the Duke's departure for England in 1798, Uniacke moved that an address and a star worth 500 guineas be presented to the Duke.[12] Before boarding his ship and before a concourse of 400 inhabitants, the presentation was duly made by Uniacke with his characteristic eloquence.

Shortly after the Duke's arrival, Uniacke was promoted to lieutenant colonel and raised a new battalion of militia, the 8th Battalion. It is unlikely that Wentworth approved and Uniacke must have had the support of the Duke of Kent. If Prince Edward had a high opinion of Uniacke's military abilities, he was soon disabused. During a military review on the King's birthday, the Duke requested Uniacke to put his battalion through a few movements. He replied "If your Royal Highness only knew how much trouble I have had in getting them into line, you would never ask me to break it".[13]

As the threat of attack from the French receded, the militia contented itself with annual musters and with being a rallying point for loyal hearts to celebrate the triumphs of British arms elsewhere in the world. Uniacke retained his command of the 8th Battalion until it was

---

12. *J.L.A.* June 30, 1798.
13. L.G. Power, "Richard John Uniacke", p. 99.

disbanded in the militia reorganization of 1820. He loved military pomp and the colours of the 8th Battalion were displayed at the Charitable Irish Society dinners, when Uniacke required his officers to turn out in dress uniform for the occasion. The 8th Battalion under his command really became the "Irish Battalion", as most of its officers were Irish and the Irish Catholic priest Edmund Burke was its chaplain.

Uniacke was, however, against any of his sons entering the regular army, and when his youngest, Andrew Mitchell, evinced a desire to do so, he did everything to discourage him. With the exception of his grandfather, other members of his family who had entered the army had never had a "Shadow of success".[14] Although, as he also told Andrew Mitchell, he had the highest regard for army officers, his long acquaintance with them had proved to him that the "military enjoy the smallest portion of happiness", being exposed to temptations and habits making them unfit "for their future state of everlasting existence". Andrew Mitchell did not go into the army, nor did he follow his father's advice and enter the church, but instead, like his father and four of his brothers, he went into law.

Under Uniacke's presidency the Charitable Irish Society thrived in the 1790's. It fulfilled his need for convivial friendship; all his close friends like Charles Hill, Charles Morris III, the Cochran and Tobin brothers, and John Pyke were members. The original articles of the society which he had drafted in 1786, had been signed by 140 Catholic and Protestant Irish Haligonians. His preamble for the revised rules in 1795 typified his romantic philosophical bent, beginning "When the helpless State of man, if left in his natural condition, is considered, he, of all Animal Creation, will be found most in want of society"; however, "by means of well regulated society weakness of man is protected, his wants are relieved, his misfortunes alleviated, and his moral nature improved". It ended on the note that the human race was but one society, and "the wants and misfortunes of every individual equally entitled to compassion and relief".[15]

St. Patrick's Day, March 17th, was the occasion for the Society's annual dinner to which were invited the governor, the presidents of the national societies and other notables. Uniacke enjoyed these occasions to the full and often gave one of the eloquent and witty speeches for which he was famous. In 1819, when replying to Judge Brenton Halliburton, who had proposed his health, he gave "a speech of great

---

14. Uniacke to his son Andrew, January 10, 1828, Vertical Manuscript File: Uniacke, Richard John, Letters to Andrew Mitchell Uniacke, P.A.N.S.

15. Records of the Charitable Irish Society, MG 20, Vol. 65, P.A.N.S.

length which commanded every feeling of his audience and kept the whole company in an uninterrupted roar of laughter".[16] Some of his speech was at the expense of Halliburton, who had just expounded upon the virtues of the Scots, claiming that there were no beggars in Scotland. Uniacke replied that he could readily understand why there were no beggars in Scotland, because everyone knew it was useless to ask charity of a "Scotchman". This dinner began in mid-afternoon and ended at dawn the following day; as was the custom, no member left until the president, who on this occasion was Uniacke's son, Richard John the younger, had departed with the guests.

Uniacke also joined the Masonic Order sometime in the 1780's. He belonged to the Grand Lodge and in all probability it was Parr, as Grand Master, who had drawn him into the order. In 1792 he was elected a worshipful master and three of his sons later joined. Feasts of the order were apparently great occasions and Uniacke was never one to miss such events. Most government officials and merchants were members, and Parr, Bulkeley and Wentworth became grand masters in succession. As the masons are a secret order, nothing is known of Uniacke's masonic activities, but the fellowship and probably also the ritual must have attracted him.

In the decade before the turn of the century, Uniacke continued to prosper, but he also spent. In 1786 he had purchased four lots on Argyle Street, the most fashionable street in Halifax. Sometime after, probably in the early 1790's, he built a three-story Georgian mansion at the corner of Argyle and Sackville Streets.[17] He needed a large home to house his family of nine children (three more were to come), his in-laws and Irish servants. He entertained much and the house and its furnishings were expensive. By 1798 he was hard pressed to find funds to send his eldest son, Norman, to London to study law at Lincoln's Inn. However, the necessary means were found, partly from his speculative backing of Simeon Perkins' privateering ventures. His law practice was also lucrative and by the mid 1790's had become the largest in Nova Scotia. The office of the solicitor general provided Uniacke with no more than two or three hundred pounds a year, but the prestige and influence associated with it drew the clients to his practice. For lawyers in colonial Nova Scotia, "place" and "practice" went together. As William Blowers Bliss, a future puisne judge, told his brother, "I

16. Ibid, and L.G. Power, "Richard John Uniacke", pp. 112-3.
17. In 1872 the house was sold and became Mumford's Market and Hotel. Today the Halifax Herald Building stands on the site.

should care less for place if I could get practice without it".[18] The expected promotion to attorney general was becoming more important than ever to his livelihood and social status. Although his claims to be promoted were superior to any other member of the Nova Scotian Bar, he feared that when the office became vacant his loyalist enemies would influence the British government to have one of their own supersede him.

Word of Chief Justice Strange's resignation arrived on June 2nd, 1797. It was accepted that Blowers would succeed him, thus opening up the attorney generalship. Within a day both Uniacke and Wentworth were writing letters to the Colonial Office, Uniacke to Portland, the Secretary of State for War and the Colonies and Wentworth to his friend John King.[19] In his letter Uniacke reiterated the promise of the attorney generalship that Lord George Germain had made him in 1780, claiming he should succeed by seniority. In addition he had been practicing at the bar longer than anyone else and had the most extensive practice. He reminded Portland that his family had uniformly supported the English connection in Ireland and had always been zealous adherents of the Crown. Portland was well aware of the Uniacke family loyalty. A cousin of Uniacke's had married the Marquis of Waterford who was Portland's brother-in-law. Others to whom Uniacke referred him were the Earl of Shannon, Lord Longueville, an Irish peer, and his school friend Sir Richard Musgrave, a member of the Irish parliament and well known politicial writer. Portland could not but be very conscious of the importance of maintaining the loyalty of families like the Uniackes in an Ireland that was rapidly moving to outright rebellion.

Uniacke in his memorial then made the extraordinary statement that he had the support of Governors Hamond, Parr and Wentworth and also of resigning Chief Justice Strange. The reference to Hamond and Parr is understandable, although Parr was of course dead, but there is a machiavellian touch to the inclusion of Wentworth and Strange. Wentworth may have intimated to Uniacke that he would support him, but it seems unlikely that Uniacke would be so fooled. More likely Wentworth was simply non-committal, recognizing Uniacke's superior claims, but hoping that John King would ensure that Portland would accept his "private" recommendations. These were that Blowers should become chief justice and Sterns attorney general. In the case of Strange

---

18. William Blowers Bliss to Henry Bliss, April 14, 1831, MG 1, Vol. 1599, P.A.N.S.
19. Uniacke to Portland, June 3, 1797, CO 217, Vol. 68 and Wentworth to King, June 4, 1797, CO 217, Vol. 37, P.R.O.

there may have been some meeting of minds, as he recommended Blowers to be chief justice, but seems to have made no recommendation for the attorney generalship.[20]

Portland replied to Wentworth in a private letter in a matter of days of having received the correspondence from Uniacke and Wentworth. It is one of the sharpest rebukes to a governor of Nova Scotia on record.[21] He told Wentworth that Blowers was to succeed Strange and that "the representation I have received from Mr. Uniacke of his services ... would have obliged me to pause had I not received the King's command to express to you his opinion that hardly any consideration whatever ought to supersede such a claim as Mr. Uniacke derives from the length of his services". He directed Wentworth to recommend Uniacke as attorney general, and "your friend Mr. Sterns" as solicitor general, informing him that any other order of succession would have forced Uniacke's resignation and affected his practice. Portland concluded by telling Wentworth that "the whole tenor of your conduct forbid my supposing that you can have seen this measure in the light in which it appears to me, & in which it would strike every professional & political man in this Kingdom". Wentworth lost no time in making the necessary arrangements and informed Portland that he had assured Uniacke "of my cordial support and influence"; to King he wrote that he had avoided relating the reasons of his former preference, as "they are all buried and I look forward to Mr. Uniacke being a very useful appointment".[22] Uniacke had also written to the Earl of Shannon, but his support was unnecessary, as Portland had already appointed Uniacke. Portland, however, told the Earl that "the interest your Lordship takes in every event which can concern the House of Uniacke would be a very powerful inducement to me to pay every attention to his, Mr. Uniacke's promotion and advancement".[23] Uniacke received a copy of Portland's letter to the Earl of Shannon; it was not the last intervention by the Shannon family on behalf of Uniacke and his sons.

Wentworth knew when he was beaten. He now decided that for the sake of the necessary harmony in the government there would have to

20. Strange to King, April 5, 1797, CO 217, Vol. 37, P.R.O. Strange also wrote Blowers to tell him of his support, See Blowers to King, March 7, 1798, CO 217, Vol. 69, P.R.O.

21. Portland to Wentworth, private. July 13, 1797, CO 217, Vol. 68, P.R.O.

22. Wentworth to Portland, September 1, 1797, private and Wentworth to King, September 10, 1797, private CO 217, Vol. 37, P.R.O.

23. Portland to Shannon, London, Wednesday night, July 19, 1797, enclosure in Uniacke to Castlereagh, June 8, 1807, CO 217, Vol. 81, miscellaneous, P.R.O.

be a reconciliation. In an attempt to remove the animosity between Uniacke and Sterns, he held a meeting between them and their friends, and presumably all agreed to behave themselves. Some time after, however, Uniacke had a street fight with Sterns, who was a weak and sickly man, and this fight may have contributed to his death in May of 1798.[24] Blowers was furious at the beating that his protegé had received and immediately challenged Uniacke to a duel. The challenge was accepted, but the city magistrates intervened, and Halifax was denied the spectacle of the chief justice and the attorney general fighting a duel. They were simply bound over, as before in 1791, to keep the peace.

The story of the street fight and the challenge was not written down until over eighty years later, by a loyalist descendant. There is no evidence of any legal action being taken against Uniacke for having beaten Sterns, and it is quite possible that the story was embellished with time. In a letter to his eldest son a few months after the fight, Uniacke revealed his attitude towards this incident: " . . . he who lives an honourable life will never be under the necessity to draw his sword in support of his reputation, for the fear of the sword may prevent a person from speaking it never will from thinking".[25]

Wentworth's failure to have his recommendation accepted for the attorney generalship was the first sign that the British government was becoming less than happy with his governship. And by gaining the place, Uniacke had won a major victory. Never again did his loyalist enemies impute insidious and disloyal motives to him. Wentworth's relations with the assembly deteriorated from this period; he came more and more to need Uniacke and to rely on him. However, Uniacke's past experience had given him no reason to trust Wentworth. As long as Wentworth was governor, no positions would be open to Uniacke's sons. He therefore lost no opportunity to let the British government know of his disapproval of Wentworth's governorship.

By 1801 Wentworth was no longer "the Sovereign's fav'rite and the subject's pride"[26] and was in such ill favor that Portland considered

---

24. The story of the beating of Sterns and the resulting challenge to a duel by Blowers was given by William John Stirling, a descendant of the Nova Scotia loyalist Thomas Hutchinson, to Peter Orlando Hutchinson who published it in his *The Diary and Letters of His Excellancy Thomas Hutchinson*, Esq. (Houghton, Miffin & Co., Boston, 1884) p. 342. James Stewart, a loyalist anxious to succeed to the solicitor generalship, reported to the Colonial Office two weeks before Sterns died that he was at the point of death; however he made no mention of the cause of the illness.

25. Uniacke to his son Norman, November 1, 1798, MG 1, Vol. 926, No. 99, P.A.N.S.

26. *On Seeing His Excellancy Sir John Wentworth Passing Through Granville* . . . by Senex, cited in Beamish Murdoch, *History of Nova Scotia*, Vol. III, p. 139.

recalling him. Since the late 1790's, in fact, there had been developing a private and public assault on Wentworth's governorship. The first straw in the political wind was the return of Charles Morris to the assembly in a by-election in 1797. Uniacke also returned to public life a year later. Secure in his appointment as attorney general, and undoubtedly aware of the change in Wentworth's fortunes, he had no hesitation in returning to the assembly when the opportunity came.

One of the representatives for Queens County had left the province and Simeon Perkins and his Liverpool friends were looking for a successor. Perkins had close business ties with the Halifax merchant brothers, the Cochrans, and it was they who suggested that Uniacke be approached. Uniacke agreed and Perkins arranged for the election to be uncontested.[27]

Two months later Perkins and some of his friends dined with Uniacke in Halifax and Perkins felt that "Mr. Uniacke appears Very well pleased & is very Sociable & easy of access to our people."[28] The relationship was strengthened by Uniacke's support for their privateering ventures. As advocate general he arranged for quick condemnation of the prizes in the Vice Admiralty Court, or as Perkins phrased it, "Mr. Uniacke was very clever in the Business".[29]

Uniacke took his seat as an ordinary member but was soon back in his speaker's chair. His election during the 1799 session to succeed the retiring Thomas Barclay was unopposed. The Uniacke who once again became speaker was more mature and self-confident than the one of ten years earlier. While, as he told his son Norman, he did not now expect to make a fortune, he was prospering. He had the respect of most (albeit by some grudgingly given) and the friendship of many. Passions had cooled, and though they were to flare up again occasionally, the sheer hatred of former days was absent.

During this session the council renewed its claim to an equal right with the assembly to frame and amend money bills. The assembly unequivocally rejected this, but on Uniacke's urgings attempted to come to an understanding. In the resultant protracted session, Uniacke, from the speaker's chair, took the initiative by drafting a resolution detailing the position of the assembly. It began by warning the council

---

27. C.B. Fergusson, ed., *The Diary of Simeon Perkins, 1797-1803* (Champlain Society, Toronto, 1967) April 25, 1798, pp. 91-2. Perkins was most happy to have "a man of Such Influence, & ability, as Mr. Uniacke" to accept the offer to represent Queens County. Perkins to Capt. Patrick Doran, April 9, 1798, C.B. Fergusson, *The Diary of Simeon Perkins 1804-1812* (Champlain Society, 1978) p. 455.

28. *Ibid.*, June 24, 1798, p. 103.

29. *Ibid.*, September 18, 1798, p. 122.

of the ill consequences of the "misunderstandings" which could interrupt all future sessions if the issue was not quickly resolved. The solution was to adhere to the usage and customs of both houses. This Uniacke argued, supported the contention of assembly that the council could not originate or amend money bills; it could only reject or agree to them. With a rhetorical flourish he told the council that the assembly would never "surrender the privileges transmitted by their ancestors".[30]

Like all common law lawyers, Uniacke had studied William Blackstone's *Commentaries on the Laws of England*. His constitutional thinking was molded by Blackstone's description of the British constitution. It was a rigid and legalistic description in which the executive, legislative and judicial functions were clearly separated, with their rights and powers defined by practice. The persuasive influence of Blackstone accounts for Uniacke's unequivocal declaration in the resolution that it was "the sole inherent and inalienable right of the Representatives of the People to frame and originate all money bills, that it is by the Law and constitution of Great Britain so established from time immemorial". If this was not enough, he told the council that whatever its claims, these could not "change that which is already fixed and established". The revenue and appropriations bills were passed without the assembly conceding the council's claim. In future disputes the assembly never deviated from this declaration of its rights given in Uniacke's resolution.

The Seventh Assembly was dissolved and the writs issued for an election in October 1799. Uniacke came under much pressure to run in Halifax County, but considered himself bound to Queens County. The Halifax County elections were shaping up as the major battleground and Uniacke also did not want to engage in a contested election. As he wrote Perkins, "I am a great enemy to Contested Elections.... having Already seen so many Evil Consequences arise from Controversies of that Kinde....". Uniacke, now nearly fifty and becoming more conservative, had no desire to engage in a contest that showed every sign of being a replay of the Morris-Sterns battle of the previous decade. He asked Perkins to "Adjust the Representation of your place in a way such as will be most acceptable as well as beneficial to the people & so as

---

30. *J.L.A.* July 4, 1799. It is not absolutely certain that Uniacke was the author; however the style and wording suggest very much that he was. The resolution had to be the work of a lawyer immersed in Blackstone and the only other lawyers in the assembly in July 1799 were James Stewart and John George Pyke, neither of whom seems the probable author.

to preclude the possibility of Controversy."[31] This Perkins did and Uniacke was again elected without opposition. Uniacke had every reason to eschew a contested election in which vast quantities of rum and the hiring of your own gang of ruffians to intimidate the voters would have been a necessity for victory. Thirty years later Joseph Howe referred to "the lawless mob dominion by which the Hustings at Halifax, and other places have been distinguished."[32]

The newly elected assembly had its first session in 1800; it was very different from its predecessor. Wentworth's web of patronage could not extend into the Eighth Assembly. He was sixty-three, often ill and in increasing disfavour in London. His authority was slipping. To regain it, he engaged in a series of confrontations with the assembly. They ended in his humiliation and the assembly's control over money bills.

The first session began with the election of Uniacke as speaker. The other nominee was William Cottnam Tonge, the representative from Halifax County whom Wentworth counted as his major enemy.[33] Wentworth charged that Tonge had "violently endeavored to supplant" Uniacke as speaker, a position he had "repeatedly filled with due ability and credit."[34] Uniacke was no doubt none too pleased at Tonge's challenge, but the speakership was no longer of much personal importance. He knew he could have a council seat when he wanted one, and Wentworth recommended him on a number of occasions. However, Uniacke refused to become a member of Wentworth's council, and by 1802 the Colonial Office was not anxious for him to be promoted because of the "advantage the Public Service derives from the able manner in which he conducts the business of the Assembly as its Speaker."[35] The journals of the house and council were sent to London and the Colonial Office seems to have been remarkably well informed about the happenings in Nova Scotia. Uniacke's great ambition was to become chief justice, and he was determined to lay a good foundation for his family with the British government to ensure that appointments would be forthcoming for his sons. Self-interest dictated that his conduct as speaker should meet with approval in London. Pride and

---

31. Uniacke to Perkins, October 12, 1799, MG 1, Vol. 980, No. 21, P.A.N.S.

32. *Novascotian*, January 16, 1834.

33. For the Wentworth-Tonge feud see Margaret Ells, "Governor Wentworth's Patronage", pp. 65-73.

34. Wentworth to King, February 23, 1800, CO 217, Vol. 37, P.R.O.

35. Unsigned to Wentworth, No. 9 (Draft), 1 December, 1802, Downing Street, CO 217, Vol. 77, P.R.O. The letter referred to the "distinguished merit of Mr. Uniacke".

self-interest also dictated that he use his growing influence to secure the removal of Wentworth, but to do so privately.

Uniacke had every reason to use his position and influence to ensure that disputes between the assembly and the council should not get out of hand, as had happened in the early 1790's. This determination was never better expressed than in his end-of-session message to Wentworth in 1800. The controversy over appropriations had continued unabated from the previous session, and Uniacke bluntly told Wentworth "that nothing but a Zealous Attachment to his Majesty's Government, and a Thorough Conviction of the Impropriety of Agitating a Question at the present Moment, which would disturb the Public Mind" could have induced the assembly to pass the revenue bill that year.[36] He then skillfully attacked Wentworth's governorship by remarking on "the decayed and ruined State of the Fisheries of the Province, and the total want of Roads of [sic] Communications between the Settlements on the Shore". The best endeavours of the assembly, he concluded, had not been able to do anything "for the Accomplishment of Objects of such great public Utility". By the directness of his address, Uniacke was warning the British government that all was not well in Nova Scotia. Wentworth immediately wrote Portland defending his council; on Uniacke's address he wrote: "individually the Speakers & I do not find that it has since been commended by the approbation of the public or Members of the Assembly".[37]

The address certainly did reflect the growing disapprobation with Wentworth. His recognition of this may have had a salutory affect, as both the 1801 and 1802 sessions were relatively quiet. The controversy over money bills, however, broke out anew during the 1803 session. The appropriations bill only passed when Uniacke as speaker cast the deciding vote.[38] Presenting the bill for Wentworth's signature provided Uniacke with the occasion to deliver another address. The war against France had broken out again, and Uniacke began by affirming the loyalty of Nova Scotians, although they were "surrounded by temptations and dangers". He then observed how the assembly had conducted its proceedings with "prudence amd moderation"; even to the point of sacrificing its feelings to preserve harmony with the council.[39] Uniacke was subtly informing the British government that it

---

36. *J.L.A.*, May 2, 1800.

37. Wentworth to Portland, May 24, 1800, RG 1, Vol. 53, No. 67, P.A.N.S.

38. B. Murdoch, *History of Nova Scotia*, Vol. III, p. 229.

39. *J.L.A.*, July 28, 1803.

was Wentworth and his council who must account for the disagreements over money bills.

Until the session of 1804 the council and assembly had really been no more than sparring. However, Wentworth and his council now made a determined effort to claim control over the expenditure of all public funds. The assembly could never accept that. The power over the public purse would pass to the executive over which the representatives of the people could have no control. A stalemate ensued between the assembly and the council and Wentworth in anger prorogued the assembly, thus losing the appropriations bill.

Uniacke had been speaker when the 1791 appropriations bill had been lost and he knew the consequences. He also knew the mood of the assembly and even though he despised Wentworth and most of his council, he had done his utmost to warn them of the consequences if they persisted in challenging the rights of the assembly. When the assembly met again in 1805, Uniacke submitted his resignation as speaker; he had a six-month leave of absence to go to England and Ireland. It was the end of a long assembly career of sixteen years during which he had never been absent a day.

While in the assembly, Uniacke had never been radical in his political opinions. His one taste of revolutionary politics had cured whatever radicalism he had absorbed as a youth in Dublin and in pre-revolutionary America. Although remaining liberal in his general attitudes, he did become in the 1790's increasingly conservative in his opposition to any opinions that might, in the language of the day, be described as "speculative". In this he was influenced by the conservative reaction in England (and also among the American Federalists) to the democratic and libertarian ideas of the French Revolution.

This reaction was mirrored in the conservative attitudes of the educated class in Nova Scotia. The mild radicalism or "sparks of liberty" evinced by some loyalists had been soon cured by place or departure from the province. Events in French and British politics were avidly followed and the winds of reaction rapidly crossed the Atlantic with each arrival of the Packet. When Bishop Charles Inglis preached to both houses of the assembly in 1793, taking his text from Proverbs, "My son, fear thou the Lord and the King, and meddle not with those who are given to change",[40] this reflected not only his loyalist background, but also genuine revulsion at the excesses of the French

---

40. Sir Adams Archibald, "Life of Sir John Wentworth," p. 57.

Revolution. The scholarly Rev. Andrew Brown of the Protestant Dissenting Church in Halifax declaimed that "when the people i.e. the unprincipled and sanguinary are supreme, the bonds of society are dissolved and the malignity of the passions rages without control".[41] Self-interest dictated that Nova Scotians anxious for office should echo the reactionary attitudes which were to dominate British politics for the next thirty years. However, there is no gainsaying that the conservatism of the educated class went beyond pure self-interest and had its roots in sincerely held beliefs. The struggle between reaction and reform, which in varying degrees of intensity dominated Nova Scotian politics for the first half of the 19th century, was between an inflexible and a liberal conservatism. Neither Uniacke nor Joseph Howe believed in universal suffrage.

Revolutionary ideas did not find fertile soil in Nova Scotia, and the agitation for radical change that culminated in the 1837 Lower and Upper Canadian rebellions was not present in Nova Scotia. Uniacke's conservatism derived not from what was happening in Nova Scotia, but from an exaggerated fear of the spread of revolutionary ideas across the Atlantic to the southern and western states of the United States, peopled, as he said, with "semi barbarians" who would overwhelm conservative New England. It would be only a matter of time before British North America would be infected and conquered. In the next thirty years he used every opportunity to arouse the British government to take measures to avert the coming disaster he so vividly and so fearfully foresaw. The measures he proposed, although radical and prescient, were rooted in his conservative philosophy.

The publication in 1805 of what are still commonly referred to as Uniacke's Laws provided him with an opportunity in the preface to warn his fellow Nova Scotians of the dangers of revolutionary ideas and didactically to remind them how fortunate they were to belong to the British Empire. The preface was more than a homily on loyalty; it was a statement of Uniacke's conservative credo.

> It has been our misfortune to live at a period, during which every art has been used to destroy the principles of true religion, and to subvert the rules of civil government. The Christian religion, which is our sure guide to the worship of the true God; the allegiance of subjects to the King; the natural love of our country; the union of husband and wife; the duties of parent and child; the affection of brothers and sisters; and the attachment of friends and countrymen, have been, by impious and wicked men, styled prejudices originating in the

---

41. Rev. Andrew Brown, D.D., *The Perils of the Time, and the Purposes for which they are appointed. A Sermon, preached on the last Sabbath of the Year 1795, and Published at the Request of the Hearers* (Halifax, 1795) p. 17.

human mind from the errors of a false education... To give the name of a
revolution to the events which have sprung from those novel doctrines, would be
applying a term too feeble to comprehend the horrid and sanguinary actions of
the apostles of liberty and equality... I think I do not exaggerate when I say,
that those diabolical principles, during the short period I advert to, have
produced to the world more human weaknesses, distress, and misery, than any
equal space of time has exhibited in the previous history of man.[42]

He ridiculed philosophers, as "enemies of the human race", who
contended that children should be taught nothing but what their reason
could comprehend. Such an education would make men "slaves of their
passions" and perpetrators of every "species of wickedness". His belief
in the importance of early instilling in children, by precept and
example, the principles of religion and morality guided him in the
education of his own children. It also caused him to fight with all his
characteristic, but impolitic, tenacity for control of education by the
Church of England.

Each member of the assembly received a copy of the Laws and for
nearly half a century it remained the standard reference. The
painstaking effort necessary in compiling all the legislation passed from
1758 to 1804 gave Uniacke a thorough knowledge of the laws of Nova
Scotia. He also had a prodigious legal memory. As one contemporary
remarked, "it seemed as easy for him to speak as to breathe. I recollect
hearing him speak for about four hours, without intermission, in a law
argument during which he cited about fifty or more cases".[43] His
imposing presence, his eloquence and his legal knowledge all combined
to give the office of attorney general, a position he held longer than
anyone else, a dignity and influence that it had never had before.
W.H.O. Haliburton, the father of the author Thomas Chandler
Haliburton, once remarked in the assembly that even if he disagreed
with one of Uniacke's legal opinions, "he would attend to the opinion of
the Attorney General who had made law his study from infancy".[44]

By 1805 Uniacke had every reason to believe that his faithful
service to the Crown, the prominent position he had attained in Nova
Scotia, and the support of his Irish patrons would ensure that his
requests for offices for his sons would receive favourable attention in
London. His decision to go to England in late 1805 was taken with the
intention of submitting his requests in person.

---

42. *The Statutes at Large passed in the several General Assemblies held in his Majesty's
Province of Nova Scotia...* by Richard John Uniacke (Halifax, 1805).

43. J.G. Marshall, *A Brief History of Public Proceedings and Events... in the Province of
Nova Scotia* (Halifax, N.S., n.d.), p. 4.

44. Assembly debates, *The Free Press*, March 9, 1819.

The responsibilities of a large family were weighing heavily on him. Martha Maria had died in 1803, leaving him to care for eleven children, three of whom were under ten. He had been absolutely devoted to her and ever after he reserved the day of her death for the consideration of "affairs little connected with this world".[45]

A few months before his departure, there was a triple wedding of Uniackes. On May 3rd, 1805, the anniversary of his own and Martha Maria's wedding, his eldest daughter Mary married Vice Admiral Sir Andrew Mitchell, his second daughter Martha Maria married Thomas Jeffery, and his second son Crofton married Dorothea Fawson. The weddings took place in St. Paul's, and Uniacke would have spared no expense to turn the affair into a gala event. Shortly after Alexander Croke, the insufferable judge of the Vice Admiralty Court, lampooned the triple wedding in his satric poem on Halifax society.

> Three blooming brides in honey moon elate
> Like Venus' Graces, round the Goddess wait;[46]

His eldest son Norman had already been admitted to the Nova Scotia bar, and had been diligently studying law in London since 1798. Shortly before his father arrived he had been admitted to Lincoln's Inn, the second native Nova Scotian to be admitted to the English Bar. His father ensured that not only had Norman had the best education available in Nova Scotia before sending him to England, but that he should also have the best legal training to fit him for office. Upon Norman's departure for London he wrote him a lengthy letter laying down "for a beloved son just entering into the world such rules and instructions as will, if adhered to, secure to him happiness and prosperity in this world".[47] Much of the letter was taken up with advising Norman on how to conduct himself in society, to manage his finances, and to resist the temptations of London. On the last score he was exhorted to "avoide with the most careful attention the misuse of wine" and "to prevent the progress of loathsome disease" by spending his leisure time in the company of "virtuous and modest women". In the choice of young company he was to be very cautious, for the "rich

---

45. Uniacke to Lord Dalhousie, February 9, 1818, Dalhousie Papers, A 527, P.A.C.

46. For the poem and its background see Thomas B. Vincent, 'The Inquisition': Alexander Croke's Satire on Halifax Society during the Wentworth Years, *Dalhousie Review*, Vol. 53, No. 3 (Autumn, 1973) pp. 404-30. The poem was first circulated in hand written copies in the winter of 1805-06 and this seems to be the only reference to the Uniacke family. Croke's Satire was mainly directed at the character and morals of Francis Wentworth who set the tone of Halifax society, and as Vincent remarks, a society that was very much alive and viable.

47. Uniacke to his son Norman, November 1, 1798, MG 1, Vol. 926, No. 99.

entice you into expense and when they see you ruined by vying with them will only laugh at your folly[,] the poor again will if possible live at your expense". On the matter of his chosen profession "no man will be a good lawyer unless he is a good man and of the professions in life which a man undertakes there is none which requires more circumspection than that of a lawyer".

The letter was filled with admonitions stressing Norman's duties to his family. Behind these was Uniacke's anguished remembrance of his own fateful break with his father. Norman was told that he was to spend his vacations in Ireland, where his aunt would inform him "with sorrow the melancholy tale of my youthfull folly". His fear that for all his efforts Norman might act towards him as he had done to his father caused him to end on a note of threatening severity.

> I feel the justice of my father's judgement & have full as much spirit as he had to resent the want of attention in a child. The want of tenderest affection for my father through every moment of his life, is I thank God what I have not to reproach myself for but for [sic] the want of attention to his admonitions & will I was justly punished. Be therefore dutifull & circumspect in your conduct by every act in your power preserve the affections of your parents & God will Bless you for it.

Norman was instructed to go to Ireland for reasons other than a family visit. He was encouraged by his father to "leave no opportunity to get introduced to the acquaintance of those who are in situations of life to be useful to you on future occasions". His Irish relations had it in their power to introduce him to some of "the first people" there and in England, which would be of immense advantage to him. In this Norman heeded his father's advice; by the time Uniacke arrived in the beginning of 1806, the Earl of Shannon had already interceded on Norman's behalf and arranged for him to be introduced to the Earl of Camden, Secretary of State for War and the Colonies, and to William Pitt during the latter's Second Administration. He had been encouraged to expect an appointnent; when Uniacke arrived in 1806 Castlereagh had become secretary of state and the Earl of Shannon arranged for an introduction. Castlereagh, who had been so instrumental in bringing about the legislative union of Ireland and England after the United Irishmen Rebellion, had every reason to view with favour requests from a member of an Irish family whose loyalty to the English connection had been so staunch.[48] Uniacke probably

---

48. During the 1798 Irish Rebellion, Uniacke's second cousin, Jasper Uniacke, and his wife were brutally murdered. He was one of the most active magistrates in County Cork and his murder received much publicity. See J.A. Froude, *The English in Ireland*, Vol. 3 (New York, 1874) p. 297. Castlereagh would undoubtedly have known of the murder and of the support accorded the Crown by the Uniacke family.

secured the promise of the Nova Scotian provincial secretaryship for Norman on the first vacancy. However, shortly after Uniacke's interview with Castlereagh, the government fell and the Ministry of All Talents came into office with William Windham as Secretary of State for War and the Colonies. It is doubtful if Uniacke's Irish patrons could have done much for him with the new ministry.

Before Uniacke's arrival, Norman had been consulted about his father's promotion to the council. Wentworth had again recommended him; Scrope Bernard, the provincial agent, was first consulted. Realizing that Uniacke would probably decline, he suggested that an arrangement be made whereby he receive precedence over future appointees when he should be promoted. He knew of "no other way of being secure from giving umbrage to a worthy public character, whose merit Mr. Cooke [the undersecretary] seems rightly to appreciate".[49] Bernard approached Norman who was of the opinion that his father did not wish to be a member of the council.[50] Later Uniacke was more explicit giving as his reason that he did not agree to many measures adopted by Wentworth.[51] The precedence arrangement was agreed to and Wentworth was duly informed by the Earl of Camden that Uniacke had been passed over in order that he might continue as speaker.[52]

Wentworth made no objection to the precedence arrangement, but his attitude would have been different if he had known that, without his knowledge, Uniacke had drafted new regulations for the disposal of crown lands in Nova Scotia. In 1790 the British government had ordered that no more land be granted, with the intention of stopping abuses and selling the lands to recover the costs of settling the loyalists. In July 1806 Uniacke was examined by the Committee of the Privy Council for Trade and Plantations.[53] Its president, Lord Aukland, had Uniacke draft a new set of regulations that would allow lands to be granted once again, with provisions to guard against abuses. Uniacke had considerable difficulty in convincing the committee that the granting of land was essential to settlement and should be allowed. His

---

49. Scrope Bernard (provincial agent) to Adam Gordon, May 2, 1805, CO 217, Vol. 80, miscellaneous, P.R.O.

50. Ibid., May 20, 1805.

51. Extract from a letter from Uniacke to Brickwoods Daniel & Co. Halifax, October 26, 1808, CO 217, Vol. 84, P.R.O.

52. Camden to Wentworth, No. 6 (Draft) July 3, 1805, CO 217, Vol. 80, P.R.O.

53. Presentations from the Lords of the Committee of Council concerning the granting of land in Nova Scotia and New Brunswick, at Queen's Palace, July 2, 1806, CO 217, Vol. 80, miscellaneous, and Uniacke to Crofton Uniacke, January 15, 1814 enclosure in Sherbrooke to Bathurst, January 19, 1814, CO 217, Vol. 94, P.R.O.

representations were accepted and the final instructions differed little from his draft. The new regulations limited grants to no more than 500 acres without the approval of the secretary of state, with no fees charged for grants under 200 acres. The fees charged for grants over 200 acres were to be used to compensate the officer appointed to keep the records. He recommended that Crofton be given this new position; however, he was told that the office would be the governor's gift. It is unlikely that Wentworth would have bestowed it on young Uniacke, but matters resolved themselves. Wentworth highly disapproved of the instructions and declined publishing them. But when Sir George Prevost was appointed to succeed him in 1808 they were immediately published, and Crofton Uniacke was made Receiver General of Quit Rents.

During this trip in 1806, Uniacke decided to visit his birthplace in Castletown, Ireland. After his absence of twenty-six years, he was not recognized even by his elder brother. He apparently met James casually and entered into conversation. Eventually, the subject of Richard John Uniacke was mentioned and he identified himself to James. He had first left Ireland as a young man with no prospects and he had now returned in middle age confident in his success and abilities. In the intervening years the vissicitudes of life had not always been kind to him, but he had overcome them and could assure his relations that he had upheld the honour of the Uniacke family.

While he was away, the election for the Ninth Assembly had been held, but he does not seem to have had any desire to return to the assembly. If he had, it is likely that he could have again been elected unopposed. Wentworth was becoming increasingly paranoid, and when William Cottnam Tonge was elected speaker in the 1806-07 session, Wentworth refused to accept him. This was an exercise of the royal prerogative unprecedented since the time of the Stuarts, but the assembly rather tamely accepted it, and elected Lewis Morris Wilkins to replace Tonge. However, when the house declared the seat of Thomas Walker of Annapolis (a friend of Wentworth's) vacant and Wentworth refused to issue a new writ, it fought back.

Wentworth had challenged the very constitutional basis of the assembly. At stake was whether the law of parliament could be transferred or vested in the Nova Scotian assembly or was the assembly simply a creature of the royal instructions and regulated by the laws of the province. As the assembly had not backed down and reinstated Walker, Wentworth and his council realized they would have to seek approval for his action in London, and as a first step, the opinion of the Nova Scotian law officers would have to be sought. In one of his most important and forceful opinions, citing cases going back to 1338, Uniacke held the assembly had acted legally in declaring Walker's election void, for he had never heard it doubted that the "Common Law of England extended to all her colonies". The Crown had granted Nova Scotia the power of legislating for itself and its assembly was "governed by the *Lex et Consuetudo Parliamenti*", and as a consequence only it could decide on the validity of Walker's election.[54]

Uniacke had written his opinion, not for the benefit of Wentworth and his council, but so that it might be submitted to the secretary of state. Before dispatching Uniacke's opinion Wentworth turned to Blowers for a contrary one. Whereas Uniacke had held the *Lex et Consuetudo Parliamenti* applied to Nova Scotia, Blowers claimed the law of parliament was peculiar to England and could not be transferred to the Nova Scotian assembly which owed its creation to the royal intructions and was regulated by the laws of the province.[55] The two opinions were sent to Castlereagh in July 1807 and he requested the law officers of the Crown give their opinion.

The assembly met again in January 1808 and the committee of the house on privileges took up the question. Foster Hutchinson, its chairman, requested of Uniacke the procedures he had followed for declaring a seat vacant when he was speaker. Uniacke replied that he never considered it part of his duty to state to the governor the reasons which caused the assembly to declare an election void.[56] The committee also received a copy of Uniacke's opinion to the secretary of state. It prepared an address protesting Wentworth's action, but by then the law officers in London had upheld the right of the assembly to decide on the validity of elections.[57] Uniacke's opinion had been instrumental in preserving the assembly's rights. It had been written from a deep knowledge of British constitutional history and the firm conviction that the Nova Scotian constitution derived its sanction from the British. The rights of Englishmen applied no less in Nova Scotia; for him Nova Scotia was not so much a colony as a partner in a great empire. Both Wentworth and Blowers had been humiliated and Uniacke's stature among his peers had risen accordingly.

As soon as it was knowledge in Halifax that the Ministry of All Talents had collapsed and Castlereagh had returned to office, Uniacke

---

54. Minutes of the Council, April 28, 1807, RG 1, Vol. 214, P.A.N.S.
55. Ibid.
56. Uniacke to Foster Hutchinson, 13 January 1808, RG 5, Series A, Vol. 14, P.A.N.S.
57. Minutes of Council, March 2, 1808, RG 1, Vol. 214, P.A.N.S.

wrote him to solicit the provincial secretaryship for Norman.[58] The incumbent, Benning Wentworth, he told Castlereagh, was dying, was incapable of performing the duties and had never possessed the necessary abilities for the office in the first place. Uniacke offered to pay an annuity for life to B. Wentworth equal to his salary, if Norman should succeed to the office. Governor Wentworth had dismissed Tonge from the naval office and Uniacke wanted this office and the provincial secretaryship united. This arrangement would have given Norman a salary of £440 plus fees of around £500 and would have made him one of the highest paid officials in the province. Uniacke attacked Wentworth for favouring his relations and fellow Americans; a native of the old country had little hope of promotion under his administration. His own appointment as attorney general, he claimed, had been the last received by an non-American. He enclosed the 1797 letter of the Duke of Portland to the Earl of Shannon and reminded Castlereagh that "My friends and relations in Ireland take a warm interest in the accomplishments of my son's views".

For one official to superannuate another so that his son could succeed to office was perhaps even too much for Castlereagh. He did write Uniacke promising that his son would have the office when B. Wentworth died. This Wentworth obiligingly did a year later, and Uniacke immediately wrote Castlereagh of his promise. The letter was a biting attack on Wentworth's governship.[59] He decried the lack of ability present in Wentworth's appointments as having a "lamentable tendency to reduce and weaken the government, the strength of which in this country depends more on public opinion that perhaps in almost any other cause". It was the continguity of the United States with its elective system that made it essential that offices not be given to improper and ignorant persons. Charging that Wentworth had been allowed more patronage than any other preceding governor for thirty years, he recommended such patronage be restored to the British government. Governors should not be allowed to remain too long in a colony as this introduced "a low venal system of corruption & favour".[60]

What Uniacke did not know, nor anyone else in Nova Scotia, was

---

58. Uniacke to Castlereagh, June 8, 1807, CO 217, Vol. 82, miscellaneous P.R.O.

59. Uniacke to Castlereagh, March 22, 1808, CO 217, Vol. 84, miscellaneous, P.R.O.

60. Similar accusations against Wentworth were made to Castlereagh by "A Loyal Colonist", August 26, 1807, CO 217, Vol. 81, miscellaneous, P.R.O. Even Blowers as early as 1802 had reached the conclusion that Wentworth ought to go. See Blowers to Jonathan Bliss, February 3, 1802, MG 1, Vol. 1603.

that the decision to remove Wentworth had already been taken. The new governor, Sir George Prevost, arrived in Halifax just two weeks after Uniacke had written his letter, and he had to deal with the question of the provincial secretaryship. He found Wentworth had already appointed his son, Charles Mary, to the office while requesting Castlereagh's approval, an old trick of Wentworth's. Charles Mary, a pompous, lazy sprig of a young man, was in England and did not want the appointment, particularly as "his family was now completely eradicated from the continent of America".[61] George Monk, an assistant judge of the supreme court and a relation of Wentworth's, solicited the favour of the Duke of Kent to obtain the office.[62] The Duke would have recommended him but was out of favour. Monk, aware that Norman was seeking the office, considered that his own forty years of service warranted that he should receive it. Norman, he thought, could be satisfied with filling his judgeship; the suggestion itself is a commentary on the ranking of place in colonial Nova Scotia.

Uniacke of course, made known Castlereagh's promise to Prevost. However, Prevost wanted to appoint his own private secretary S.H. George, because he had no other means to provide for him. To this Castlereagh agreed and a year later appointed Norman to the attorney generalship of Lower Canada, an appointment that was to be bitterly resented there and cause much anguish to Norman and his father. Provost immediately appointed Uniacke to the council in conformity with the previously agreed arrangement for precedence, finding him to be a "Man of good estate, and good character".[63]

Uniacke remarried in 1808; his new wife was Eliza Newton, the daughter of Captain Philipps Newton of the 40th Foot. To his children he gave as his reason for remarrying the duty he owed to them and to himself.[64] She bore him one son in the first year of their marriage. Shortly after the marriage, the Uniackes attended the governor's ball. There he watched with pride while Prevost opened the gala event with Lady Mary (Uniacke) Mitchell on his arm. The Uniackes as a family had arrived and all Halifax knew it.

---

61. C.M. Wentworth to Captain Dodd (secretary to the Duke of Kent) April 26, 1808, Monk Family Papers, microfilm, reel 4, P.A.C. Young Wentworth thought the secretaryship was to go to Michael Wallace.

62. Judge George Monk to the Duke of Kent, April 5, 1808, ibid.

63. Prevost to Castlereagh, May 14, 1808, RG 1, Vol. 58, No. 14, P.A.N.S.

64. Uniacke to My Dear Children, November 12, 1823, Vertical Manuscript File: Uniacke, Richard John, Will, 1823, P.A.N.S.

Chapter Four

The American States... Dread the Day When the English Government Shall Turn its Thoughts to Nova Scotia

The British government seldom thought about Nova Scotia, and never so seldom as during the twenty-year war with Republican France. Other than the threatened French attack in 1793, Nova Scotians were left in peace to work out their own destiny in a world beseiged by war and revolution. During the American Revolutionary War Nova Scotians had been exhorted by Henry Alline, "the Apostle of Nova Scotia", to see themselves as a "people highly favoured of God".[1] The more distant yet seemingly nearer terrors of the French Revolutionary War evoked a similar response. This was never better expressed than in the sermon of Rev. Andrew Brown, who, after describing the evils that had befallen Europe, called upon his Halifax congregation to remember "how singularly have we been protected and preserved in this part of the empire amidst the alarming dispensations of Divine Providence?"[2]

From this belief that they were somehow divinely favoured, Nova Scotians came to have a sense of their own uniqueness as a people and their land as a special place with its own destiny. Uniacke's conviction was that Nova Scotia's destiny was to be a great maritime state. However, he did not give credit to divine providence for Nova Scotia's escape from the ravages of war and revolution, but to the protection offered by the mother country.[3]

Uniacke had an exaggerated faith in the destiny of his adopted

1. See Gordon Stewart and George Rawlyk, *A People highly favoured of God; the Nova Scotia Yankees and the American Revolution* (Macmillan of Canada, Toronto, c. 1972).

2. Rev. Andrew Brown, D.D. *The Perils of the Time, and the Purposes of which they are appointed. A Sermon, preached on the last Sabbath of the Year 1794, and Published at the Request of the Hearers* (Halifax, 1795) p. 37.

3. Preface to *The Statutes at Large ... Province of Nova Scotia* by Richard John Uniacke.

land. In his preface to his Laws he envisaged it as becoming "powerful in maritime force" and its population exceeding "any other country in America of the same extent". Nova Scotia could only achieve her destiny if her people were allowed the same commercial freedom that the Americans had gained with independence. From the early 1790's he strove with characteristic tenacity to impress upon the British government that the very contiguity of the United States made it impossible to apply the restrictive laws of trade and navigation to Nova Scotia and indeed to the whole of British North America.

His efforts to gain commercial freedom were attuned to the ambitions of the Halifax merchants who had been endeavouring since 1784 to secure commercial control over eastern British America, to make Halifax into an entrepôt of North Atlantic trade, and above all to gain the West Indian trade by having the Americans excluded from any direct intercourse with those islands.[4] Although he did not engage in mercantile pursuits himself, his relations with merchants, such as the Cochran brothers and Charles Hill, were based upon both interest and friendship. As Advocate General of the Vice Admiralty Court for over thirty years, no one gained a greater mastery over the complex and bewildering laws of trade and navigation. The mercantile interests turned to him again and again to put forward their case. He not only did so in commercial terms, but also linked commercial freedom with union of the British North American colonies. In the 1820's he set forth his vision of a great and powerful British American state whose commercial destiny would rival that of the expanding republic to the south which he both feared and envied.

The restraints on colonial trading, so much opposed by Uniacke, were part of the mélange of hundreds of acts and orders-in-council that came under the legislative umbrella of the 17th century navigation laws: a cardinal tenet was that trade between colonies and between Britain and her colonies had to be conducted in British shipping. By providing protected markets, the navigation laws did benefit the colonies, but they also made it nearly impossible to trade in foreign markets. Colonial products could not be sent directly to a foreign market. All exports and imports had to be landed in Britain for payment of duty. Foreign shipping could not enter colonial ports.

One of the causes of the American revolution had been the restraints on New England trading in foreign markets. The dilemma in

---

4. See D.A. Sutherland, "The Merchants of Halifax, 1815-1850: A Commercial Class in Pursuit of Metropolitan Status" (unpublished PhD Thesis, University of Toronto, 1975) pp. 13-16.

which Britain found itself after American independence was compounded by the long war with France. Britain wanted access to the American market; the Americans, in turn, wanted readmission into the commercial privileges of the empire. Britain, however, would not grant the latter, fearing the loss of too much of the carrying trade. The period 1783 to 1830 was one of forced commercial concessions, large scale smuggling, and war, interspersed with fluctuating periods of economic prosperity and depression for Britain, Nova Scotia and the United States.[5]

After 1783 the West Indies trade was considered crucial to all three. The aim of British policy was to exclude the United States from this trade, and to have the British North American colonies replace the United States as suppliers of fish, provisions and lumber. The ensuing struggle for the West Indian trade dominated Nova Scotian commercial life for some forty years, falling into three fairly distinct periods: from American independence to the war with France in 1793, for the duration of the war, and from the end of the war in 1815 to 1830 when American ships were admitted into the West Indian ports in exchange for the removal of discriminating duties against British ships in American ports.

Both native Nova Scotians and the arriving loyalists had anticipated that, with American independence, they would take over the West Indian trade. They saw themselves as replacing the American states as suppliers of fish, provisions and lumber and becoming an essential part of the lucrative imperial trans-Atlantic trade. But American shipping would have to be excluded from the West Indies, and only after some hesitation did parliament enact the necessary legislation. The re-established imperial monopoly worked reasonably well, but the British North American colonies found it difficult to meet West Indian demands in quality or price. The virtually unlimited access to the fisheries which had been granted the Americans after 1783 greatly hindered Nova Scotia from competing in the crucial fish trade. Shortages of provisions made it not only impossible to supply the West Indies on a regular basis, but opened up to the Americans the opportunity to engage in the smuggling of provisions and other commodities in exchange for Nova Scotian fish, which could then be smuggled into the West Indies or taken to American ports for re-export in British ships.

A proposal had been made in 1784 to make Halifax a free port by

5. For the commercial warfare of this period see Gerald S. Graham, *Sea Power and British North America, 1783-1820* (Cambridge, 1941).

allowing foreign shipping and importations. Such ships would not have been permitted to take on cargoes, however, thus making it commercially unattractive. The idea was dropped until 1791 when Uniacke, as speaker, in a letter to the provincial agent, urged him to press for Halifax to be made a free port, and hopefully turn it into an entrepôt to draw in American ships and products for exchange with British manufactures. Nova Scotian merchants could then mix native and American products for shipment to the West Indies, thereby meeting West Indian needs and dampening the mounting pressure for American direct intercourse with the islands. The plea for a free port was renewed by Uniacke a year later but the provincial agent had no success in convincing the British government.[6]

Nova Scotians were left to struggle under the restraints of the old commercial system. The outbreak of war with France in 1793 made trade with West Indies increasingly difficult. Nova Scotian vessels were subject to high insurance charges and the ravages of French privateers. The demands of war removed many British merchantmen from the trade and soon the islands were facing starvation. Their ports were opened to American shipping. Nova Scotian trade languished, her fisheries fell under American control, and her people became habituated to smuggling to survive.

By 1803 matters had come to such a pass that the provincial agent, Scrope Bernard, reported that nothing could be done while the war lasted and suggested that he not be paid. Uniacke, now again speaker, had been urging him to impress upon the British government the necessity for a complete review of the whole commercial system.[7] Bernard had approached Lord Glenbervie, Vice President of the Privy Council Committee of Trade, and he agreed with Uniacke, but the war made such an investigation impossible. Undaunted, Uniacke told Bernard not to "despond", warning him that unless Britain paid serious attention to its American fisheries, of which Nova Scotia's were the most bountiful, they would be completely lost to the Americans.

The 1783 treaty had opened the fisheries to the Americans. Uniacke wanted it either amended or the commercial system changed to give Nova Scotian merchants equal advantages for the export of fish. Crucial to the fish trade was the importation of salt, which largely came from the Mediterranean in exchange for fish. Nova Scotian merchants were prohibited from bringing back wine, fruit and other articles to

---

6. Uniacke to Richard Cumberland, August 16, 1791 and September 20, 1792, RG 1, Vol. 302, Nos. 13 and 20, P.A.N.S.

7. Uniacke to Scrope Bernard, November 29, 1803, RG 1, Vol. 303, No. 53, P.A.N.S.

make up cargoes without stopping in England and paying duties. Free from these restrictions, the Mediterranean trade fell largely into American hands. In every letter to the agent Uniacke stressed the importance of changing the system so Nova Scotians could compete in the vital salt trade. This was done finally in 1806 and marked the turning point in Nova Scotia's commercial fortunes.

Uniacke's efforts were complemented by the Halifax Committee of Merchants in 1804 which petitioned for the complete exclusion of the Americans from the West Indian trade.[8] The short peace with France had ended and the American penetration of the fisheries and the West Indian trade continued unabated. Even more galling, because American ships entered West Indian market by proclamation they paid no duty, but Nova Scotians had to pay the normal duties. Nova Scotians knew that Anglo-American commercial negotiations were underway and feared that the Americans would be granted even more privileges, thus destroying what commercial life was left. Bernard also reported that Lord Glenbervie, who was sympathetic to Nova Scotia's interests, had retired from office.

In this mood of despair and frustration, Uniacke made his decision, for personal reasons, to go home for a visit. He wrote the clerk of the house, "I flatter myself with the hope that my being on the spot will give activity to measures so highly important to the interests of this province". He intended to present "a Just & Impartial Statement of the present situation of the British Colonies & the absolute necessity there is for the Eye of Government to be turned towards objects so very important".[9] His statement or memoir was presented to the Secretary of State of Colonies and War, William Windham, just after the Ministry of All Talents had assumed office.[10] The ministry was favourable to peace with France and to commercial concessions to the Americans. Uniacke was not opposed to the former but was admantly against the latter, and in his memoir he urged the necessity for Britain to counter

8. See G.F. Butler, "The Early Organization and Influence of Halifax Merchants", *Collections*, N.S.H.S., Vol. 25, pp. 1-16.

9. Uniacke to the Clerk of the Assembly, November 9, 1805, RG 1, Vol. 303, No. 59, P.A.N.S.

10. Memoir presented to Mr. Windham, February 18, 1806, miscellaneous, CO 217, Vol. 80, P.R.O. (hereafter Memoir, 1806). See also D.C. Harvey, "Uniacke's Memorandum to Windham, 1806, Canadian Historical Review (hereafter *C.H.R.*) Vol. XVII, No. 1 (March, 1936) pp. 41-58. Harvey in publishing the manuscript used a copy held by the P.A.N.S. In places there are minor differences in wording, but not in sense, between the P.A.N.S. and P.R.O. copies. I have used the P.R.O. copy.

the rising power of the United States by encouraging the commerce of British North America.

The memoir began with an apocalytic and shrewd appraisal of the consequences of the independence of the American colonies to British power and commercial interests. Uniacke warned of the dangers of the rising power and wealth of the United States nurtured by French intrigue and the continued transfer of British capital and talents to the "pestilential & factious cities" of America. This capital would be swallowed up in the general confusion that must inevitably await a country to which could be traced the "evil principles" which had overturned the legitimate government of France.

Nova Scotians maintained close commercial and personal ties with conservative New England, which gave its support to the Federalists, the party of the commercial and propertied class. The defeat of the Federalist party and the election of the Democrats and Thomas Jefferson as president in 1800 convinced many that the end of the union was inevitable. Nova Scotians as well as conservative Americans readily agreed with the American chief justice, John Marshall, when he wrote on the morning of Jefferson's inauguration, "The Democrats are divided into speculative theorists & abstract terrorists. With the latter I am disposed to class Mr. Jefferson".[11] Uniacke, with his deep suspicion of faction, called Jefferson a "cold blooded infidel calculator",[12] and believed that the "speculative theories" upon which the American government was formed had proved unequal to contend with faction and intrigue. Now, he told Windham, was the time to recall British subjects and capital from a country where every man of property "dreads the fraternal hug of Liberty & Equality".[13]

All that was required to achieve this was for Britain to allow the British North American colonies to trade in British shipping to all parts of the world with the same freedom that American merchants enjoyed. One free port should be opened in Canada, two in Nova Scotia and one in New Brunswick, into which foreigners in their own ships would be permitted to import all the natural productions of the American States, of the West Indies and of South America, while reserving the re-exportation exclusively to British subjects and ships. American

---

11. John Marshall to C.C. Pinckney as quoted in Richard Hofstadter and others, *The American Republic*, Vol. 1 (Prentice-Hall, Englewood Cliffs, New Jersey, 1959) p. 288.

12. Uniacke to Frederick Robinson, President of the Board of Trade, November 16, 1822, Board of Trade, 6/253, p. 9, P.R.O.

13. Memoir, 1806.

goods would be drawn into the free ports for re-export to the West Indies, thus giving colonial ports a "decided superiority" over American and thereby make it in the interest of merchants to move to British America. He was in no doubt that the Americans dreaded "the day when the English Government shall turn its thoughts to Nova Scotia", well knowing that if the same commercial liberties enjoyed by the Americans were extended to Nova Scotia and the other North American colonies, American trade and capital would soon move to the colonies.

Uniacke was not arguing for an end to the old commercial system; he wanted it modified for the benefit of British America, whose proximity to the United States made it impossible for Britain to continue to maintain a monopoly of colonial trade. He could never accept that the same argument applied in equal measure to the West Indies. Their trade was to remain a monopoly for the benefit of Britain and British America. He countered West Indian arguments for the continuation of free ports thereby playing on British fears that this would inevitably lead to revolution instigated by American and French intrigues. Uniacke refused to accept that the West Indies were of much greater commercial importance than British North America, and this made him extol with missionary zeal the value of Nova Scotia as "of more importance to Great Britain than perhaps any other foreign possession belonging to the Crown". He despised the West Indian planters as a class, and he was quite prepared to sacrifice their interests to his vision of Nova Scotia as a great maritime state.

A few months after Uniacke had presented his memoir, Windham and the Ministry of All Talents fell from office. Nova Scotia's attempts to plead her case seemed ill-fated. But Uniacke had certainly made a favourable impression on officials such as Mr. Cooke, the undersecretary, and on Castlereagh, who succeeded Windham. He also impressed the publicist Nathaniel Atcheson, who in 1808 published *American Encroachments on British Rights*, quoting almost verbatim from Uniacke's memoir.[14]

Governor Sir Thomas Carleton of New Brunswick, then in England, hoped that Uniacke's representations would turn the attention of the British government to the state of colonial trade.[15] What Uniacke did achieve was to present Nova Scotia's case and that

---

14. A copy, which was inscribed by the author, was sent to Uniacke. It is in the Akins Library, P.A.N.S.

15. Lieutenant Governor Thomas Carleton to Edward Winslow, Bath, March 3, 1806, *Winslow Papers, 1776-1826*, p. 549.

of British America to the British government, and through Atcheson to a segment of the British public, in a forceful and direct manner.

The British government did finally turn its thoughts to Nova Scotia and her sister colonies; not, however, as a deliberate act to modify the old commercial system, but as a reaction to the embargo and non-intercourse acts which the Americans initiated in 1807. Britain retaliated against these measures by opening free ports in Nova Scotia and New Brunswick, thus encouraging Americans to break their own laws, which they did with alacrity. An immense smuggling trade grew up, with American vessels bringing provisions and fish into the free ports to exchange for British manufactures and West Indian rum and sugar. Nova Scotia finally became that great entrepôt for North Atlantic trade envisaged by Uniacke, and the colony prospered.

The War of 1812-14 increased this prosperity and fortunes were made in both trading and privateering. As the war forced a complete American withdrawal, American maritime expansion was checked and the fisheries made a dramatic recovery. Earlier in 1806 Nova Scotian shipping had gained the right to import wines, oranges and raisins directly from the Mediterranean, if the export product was fish, and legislation in 1815 and 1817 permitted direct trading to British colonies in the Mediterranean for most exports and imports. From 1801 to 1808 the total tonnage of ships trading to and from Nova Scotia doubled, and doubled again by 1815 to nearly 150,000 tons. Not only had trade greatly expanded, but the Americans had to pay in specie for their imports of British manufactures obtained via British America. The triumph seemed complete and prosperity gained.

Events had proved the soundness of Uniacke's advocacy of free ports, but more than free ports would be required to make Nova Scotia into a great maritime state. In his memoir Uniacke outlined the political changes he thought necessary to complement the commercial ones.

Uniacke may have quarrelled bitterly with the loyalists over patronage, but he was at one with them on the causes of the American Revolution. As they watched the struggles in the former colonies to create a nation, their personal experiences during the revolution were confirmed. The collapse of the Federalists and the triumph of Jeffersonian democracy further cemented their conservatism and loyalty to British institutions. The close ties maintained by blood and interest with secessionist-minded New England both gave support to their views and distorted the reality of what was happening. And for no one was this more true than for the pre-loyalist Uniacke. It was not the idea of union that he opposed; on the contrary, Uniacke shared the arguments of many loyalists that had a union been imposed on the colonies by the British government there would have been no rebellion.

Uniacke further believed that the breakup of old Nova Scotia into four separate "petty states" had been the result of a similarly mistaken British policy of divide and rule.[16] In his memoir he argued for New Brunswick, Prince Edward Island and Cape Breton to be reunited to Nova Scotia. (In 1784 he had been one of those who had protested the creation of New Brunswick, and Edward Winslow had then accused him of disloyalty; in 1806 Winslow saw only a degree of "impudence" in Uniacke's proposals.[17]) Uniacke also disagreed with the 1791 act which had established the Canadas, and wanted them reunited to complement the union of the maritime colonies. Each new province was to be placed under one governor and one legislature to form "two powerful Governments", which, with changes to the old commercial system, would draw in British capital and make them truly rivals of the American states.[18]

Of nothing was Uniacke more convinced than that officers of the Crown should be independent of assembly control. Their salaries should be adequate and fully paid by the Crown so they could uphold the authority of the imperial government in the colony. Uniacke was not advocating independence from assembly control as a means of consolidating the position of local colonial oligarchies;[19] rather, he wanted the imperial government to exercise much greater control over its officials. It was this very lack of control over Wentworth's appointments that drew his fiercest criticism a year later. Most of the important officials in Nova Scotia were members of the council, and because of its legislative role these officials often became

---

16. Historians have tended to agree with Uniacke on the reason for the partition of Nova Scotia. See for example, M. Gilroy, "The Partition of Nova Scotia", *C.H.R.*, Vol. XIV, No. 4 (December 1933) pp. 375-91. W.S. MacNutt, however, argues that it was the need to satisfy loyalist "amour propre" in his *The Atlantic Provinces: The Emergence of Colonial Society 1712-1857* (McClelland and Stewart, Toronto, 1965) pp. 95-7.

17. Edward Winslow to James Fraser, Kingsclear, October 12, 1806, quoting William Knox, *Winslow Papers, 1776-1826*, p. 569.

18. Memoir, 1806.

19. D.C. Harvey in his introduction to "Uniacke's Memorandum to Windham, 1806" suggests, incorrectly in my opinion, that the memoir was an example of "an intelligent local oligarchy proving its imperialism in order to win complete control of a local situation". pp. 41-2.

involved in personal controversies with the assembly. Uniacke wanted this stopped by creating a separate legislative council in which servants of the Crown would have no role.[20]

A legislative council, appointed by the governor for the duration of each assembly and not for life, as in the Canadas, would be made up of men of influence, ability and property from throughout the province who would control any "factious disposition" on the part of the assembly.[21] The membership of the privy or executive council, which would act as the governor's advisers, was to be drawn from senior officials, and from members of the assembly. In no sense did Uniacke foresee the executive council being responsible to the assembly; this was quite consistent with the English 18th century constitutional assumption that ministers were the King's servants and that the executive branch of government belonged to him alone.[22]

His memoir presented, Uniacke preoccupied himself with obtaining appointments for his sons and with visiting Ireland. A year and a half after his return to Nova Scotia, Wentworth fell from grace and was replaced by Sir George Prevost.

Prevost was the first of a succession of Napoleonic War veterans who began as governors of Nova Scotia and then were promoted to govern the troublesome Lower Canadians. His portrait by Robert Field shows him to have been a small man with a pleasing countenance. Reasonably able and conciliatory, he had been appointed to shore up the defences of Nova Scotia as war with the United States became more likely. Before his departure from England, Castlereagh had suggested that he employ Uniacke to write publications to awaken the Americans to the ill conduct and impolicy of their government and described him as "a Gentleman perfectly conversant in the manner and interests of the Eastern States, and also possessed of good Talents and Eloquence". He recommended that Prevost should call Uniacke's abilities to his assistance.[23] Prevost immediately appointed Uniacke to the council and set him to work drafting a new militia bill.

Hardly had Prevost arrived than he had to begin preparations for

---

20. The 1791 Canadas Act established for the first time a legislative council separate from the old colonial councils. See Martin Wright, *The Development of the Legislative Council 1600-1945* (Faber, London, 1946) pp. 31-2.

21. Memoir, 1806.

22. Richard Pares, *King George III and the Politicians* (Oxford, 1953) p. 97.

23. Castlereagh to Prevost, February 13, 1808, Private and Secret, CO 217, Vol. 82, P.R.O. There is no evidence that Uniacke ever wrote any pamphlets for distribution in the Eastern States.

a military expedition against Martinique in December 1809. Alexander Croke, the Judge of the Court of Vice Admiralty, would be administrator in his absence, and Prevost knew there would be trouble. Blowers was president of the council, but as chief justice he was precluded from becoming administrator, and Croke was next in precedence. Croke, whom Prevost described as a "rather unpopular character",[24] was the most disliked man in Halifax, but Prevost considered he had no choice but to appoint him. The stage was set for another constitutional row, but this one would have a different twist, for the assembly and council lined up together against Croke when he refused to sign the 1809 appropriations bill.

Croke was particularly incensed over a resolution appointing a provincial agent in London, about which he was never officially informed. Enraged at this slight, Croke refused to sign the appropriations bill, but wanted to expend the funds voted even if the bill did not become law. The council refused to sanction such expenditures and did so upon an opinion given by Uniacke as principal law officer of the Crown.[25] His main argument was that the laws of England were clear that no funds could be expended other than by an act of parliament and he considered the same laws applied in Nova Scotia.

Enraged at this slight, Croke refused to sign the appropriations bill, but wanted to expend the funds voted even if the bill did not become law. The council refused to sanction such expenditures and did so upon an opinion given by Uniacke as principal law officer of the Crown.[25] His main argument was that the laws of England were clear that no funds could be expended other than by an act of parliament and he consider the same laws applied in Nova Scotia.

Upon his return Prevost signed a new appropriations bill. This unnecessary and petty constitutional dispute did afford the opportunity for Uniacke to write the best researched argument made by any Nova Scotian upholding the constitutional principle that the laws of parliament applied in Nova Scotia. War and prosperity, however, soon supplanted constitutional issues and came to dominate provincial life.

With the prosperous times of the War of 1812 the work of the Vice Admiralty Court multiplied. Between 1792 and 1815, 700 prizes passed through the Court, at least 200 of them after 1812. Uniacke drew large

---

24. Prevost to Edward Cooke, September 23, 1808, CO 217, Vol. 83, P.R.O.
25. Opinion of the Attorney General, enclosure No. 2 in Croke to Castlereagh, April 3, 1809, CO 217, Vol. 85, P.R.O.

fees from the condemnations of these prizes and by the end of the war he had amassed a fortune of £50,000.[26]

With this large fortune he could fulfill his great dream of a country house and estate. He did not choose a location on the Halifax peninsula nor at the rural retreat of Windsor, as was the habit of wealthy Haligonians; rather, he selected a site in the wilderness on the Windsor road, twenty-five miles from Halifax. Tradition has it that when he was being escorted as a prisoner from Fort Cumberland in 1776, the party stopped at this spot. Uniacke, who was in irons, requested the sergeant, a fellow Irishman named Lawlor, to take off the shackles, pledging his honour not to escape. Lawlor did this and Uniacke, after wandering about, declared the surroundings resembled his family's estate in Ireland and swore to Lawlor that he would one day return and build a house there.[27] This story may be somewhat apocryphal, as the site bears no resemblance to the Irish Mount Uniacke, but its romanticism is typically Uniacke. Lawlor afterwards left the army and settled in Dartmouth. His family became members of the Charitable Irish Society, and when Lawlor came across the harbour for his Easter communion each year he stayed with Uniacke in Halifax.

In 1784 Uniacke was granted 1000 acres on the Windsor road. On this property he built Mount Uniacke between the years 1813 and 1815.[28] By purchase and further grants he formed an estate of over 11,000 acres, but by his own admission only 500 acres could be cultivated. Even this was an exaggeration; his lands were among the most unproductive in the province, the classic Nova Scotia mixture of swamp and rock, dying forest and sour, acid soil. Nonetheless he spent substantial sums in clearing and farming his lands, in what his family and contemporaries agreed was a most unprofitable enterprise. But his romantic instinct overrode all and to his dying day he enjoyed his dream fulfilled, a monument to his success in the New World.

The Mount itself is on a gentle slope which runs down to Lake Martha, named after his first wife. It was sited with the double purpose

---

26. See Lionel H. Laing, "Nova Scotia's Admiralty Court as a Problem of Colonial Administration, *C.H.R.*, Vol. XVI, No. 2 (June 1935) p. 161 and for the extent of his fortune, P. Lynch, "Early Reminiscences of Halifax", *Collections*, N.S.H.S., Vol. XVI, p. 191.

27. L.G. Power, "Richard John Unicake," p. 11.

28. For details concerning the land grants and construction of Mount Uniacke I am much indebted to Ms. Yvonne Piggott. In the early 1800's Uniacke considered building a country home in Windsor; see George Monk to his brother Sir James Monk, Windsor, September 2, 1802, Monk Papers, MG 23, G 11-19, Vol. 2, p. 31, P.A.C. According to Monk, Uniacke in 1802 already had a country or summer home on the Windsor road.

of giving an impressive first view of the stately portico from the road running a few yards from the house, and a beautiful prospect from the house itself, which faces south-east.[29] One Captain Fotheringay, when he first caught a view of the Mount, described it as an "enchanted palace" with "an air of beautiful romance", and was particularly fascinated by the entrance gate, which he declared was "one of the most wonderful exhibitions of taste which ever met my eyes".[30]

The house, now an historic home cared for by the Nova Scotia government, is Georgian, two storeys high, standing upon a cellar which was used as the kitchen and servants' quarters. The ground floor is divided down the centre by a hallway, a third of the width and running the full length of the house. On one side is the dining room and Uniacke's library; on the other, a drawing room and a bedroom, whose nineteenth century occupants claimed was haunted by the Old Attorney General. Upstairs there are seven bedrooms. Each room in the house was heated by a large stove instead of a fireplace. Almost all the furniture he had made to order in solid mahogany by the London cabinet maker George Adams. Even the brass hardware used on the doors matches in design that used on the furniture. The walls were enriched by family portraits, including those by Robert Field of Uniacke and his daughter Alicia. After his death portraits by John Singleton Copley and Robert Feke were added.[31] His sons, when in England, were instructed to purchase prints of famous men.

His library was his great pleasure and where he had his large chair. The room is lined with bookshelves with each book having his crested bookplate and the Uniacke motto, "Faithful and Brave". There could be no better illustration of the quality of Uniacke's mind and the range of his interests than the books themselves: history, geography, literature, the classics, religion and philosophy, law, political economy and government, everything from Voltaire's *Essay on Universal History* to a large selection on agriculture and applied science, including a

---

29. See Constance Piers, "Mount Uniacke: An Old Colonial Mansion and Its Historic Hierlooms", unpublished paper given before the N.S.H.S. March 18, 1927, MG 20, Vol. 676, No. 1, P.A.N.S. and in part published with photographs in *Canadian Homes and Gardens* (March 1927), pp. 36-7.

30. "A ride from Halifax to Windsor, a letter from Captain Fotheringay to his friend Charles Escalon", *Novascotian*, September 20, 1827.

31. For the Robert Field portrait of Uniacke see the catalogue to Robert Field Exhibition organized by the Art Gallery of Nova Scotia, Halifax, October 5 to November 27, 1978, pp. 72-3, and for Feke and Copley portraits see Marie Elwood "Two portraits attributed to Robert Feke" *The Magazine Antiques* (November, 1979) pp. 1150-52 and "Collectors' Notes", *ibid.*, January 1980, p. 221.

volume on *The Theory and Practice of Warming and Ventilating Public Buildings*.[32]

One of the first of many notable visitors was Bishop Plessis of Quebec, who in 1815 broke his journey to Windsor to spend a night at the Mount. The next morning he surveyed the "immense and costly mansion", and its numerous outbuildings, and found "baths, billard room, balconies, barns, stables, domestic quarters, arbours arranged along the banks of a pleasantly-sized lake, whose waters are led to it by brooks as to the sea; nothing had been overlooked which could render the place delightful". Remarking that £20,000 had already been spent on the estate, he commented that here mankind was displayed: "some win and some waste, the former to gratify their avarice, the latter their vanity or their pleasure, life is passed in these diverse occupations and nobody worries about eternity".[33] Uniacke did worry about eternity, but his concern did not interfere with the pleasure he derived from the Mount.

The Mount had been built as his retirement residence and upon its completion in his sixty-second year he went into semi-retirement. His large town house was available when he came to Halifax but his law practice was largely in the hands of his sons, Crofton and Richard John the younger. As attorney general he still had to go on circuit, although he gradually passed this duty over to the solicitor general. His health remained excellent and at a public subscription dinner to celebrate the victory at Waterloo, which he chaired, he and his fellow diners drank no less than 101 toasts. When he was met early next morning by a friend and asked if the dinner was just over, he answered not at all, he was going home for his snuff box and then was going back to finish the list of toasts.[34] His love of parties was undiminished, and at one given by Charles Hill a dance was suggested, but there was no musical instrument available. Uniacke said he would go over and get Nancy's spinet. Nancy lived a fair distance away and it was late, but he went over and knocked on her door saying "I'm Mr. Uniacke, the Attorney General. In the King's name open the door or I'll break it in." Nancy was delighted to hand over her spinet, whereupon Uniacke put it on his shoulders and carried it back to the Hills'.[35]

---

32. For a description of the library, see Shirley Elliott, "The Library of Richard John Uniacke 1753-1830: Attorney General of Nova Scotia", *Bulletin, Maritime Library Association*, Vol. 21, No. 2, (Winter 1957) pp. 25-8.

33. As translated in Cyril Byrne's, "The Maritime Visits of Joseph Octave Plessis, Bishop of Quebec", *Collections*, N.S.H.S., Vol. 29, pp. 41-2.

34. L.G. Power, "Richard John Uniacke", p. 112.

35. *Ibid.*, pp. 113-4.

When Prevost succeeded to the governor generalship in 1811, he was replaced in Halifax by another Napoleonic War veteran, Sir John Sherbrooke. During his five years of office, Sherbrooke proved to be the ablest of governors. Firm and fair in his dealings, he would play no favourites. Uniacke's relationship with him was never as intimate as it was with his successor Lord Dalhousie. On one occasion at a dinner party given by Sherbrooke, Uniacke, after telling a colonel one of his improbable stories, remarked "Pon my word, Colonel, I should not have believed it if I had not seen it myself". Sherbrooke interjected, "Then, Mr. Uniacke, you will pardon me if I do not believe it".[36] Sherbrooke did recommend, however, that young Richard John be made attorney general of Cape Breton. The then governor, Major General Hugh Swayne, who knew the Irish Uniackes well, readily agreed, and Richard John was duly appointed in 1814. (No doubt the two casks of old claret destined for the French ambassador in Washington and taken as a prize, which Richard John brought to Swayne as a gift from his father, served as a good an introduction as any.[37])

War had destroyed the American dominance of the fisheries and the West Indian trade. It was well understood in Halifax that, with peace, the Americans would make every effort to regain their dominant position. The Halifax Merchants' Committee of Trade petitioned in 1813 for the continued exclusion of the Americans from the West Indian trade and the fisheries. Sensing that the British government was perhaps wavering on the issue of American exclusion, Uniacke took the initiative to organize an address to the Prince Regent from the council and the assembly.[38] The address warned against any concessions to the Americans, who desired only the destruction of British commerce. The Treaty of Ghent in 1814 brought peace with the United States, but it left in abeyance the question of new commercial relations between the United States and the British colonies.

After the war importations from the United States were allowed if they were purchased by British subjects and shipped in British ships. By 1817 Halifax commission merchants were doing a roaring business and smuggling was common. When two of them petitioned that they be allowed to import directly from American merchants, their request was

---

36. *Ibid.*, p. 113.

37. Uniacke to Swayne, October 28, 1813, Brigadier General H. Swayne's Papers, p. 309, P.A.C.

38. Journals of the Legislative Council (hereafter J.L.C.) March 1-7, 1814. The ideas and language of Uniacke so permeate the address that he must have been responsible for almost the whole address.

referred to Uniacke for his opinion. Uniacke dismissed it and used the opportunity to present his ideas for changes in British colonial policy. This memorandum was sent to the Board of Trade and seems to have been of some influence in having free ports opened in 1818.[39] It had arrived in London just when the Americans were launching another series of measures designed to break Britain's monopoly of her colonial trade.

In his memorandum Uniacke, with astonishing prevision, confidently assumed an imperial partnership in which the mother country and "her Foreign Dominions" were not only tied by affection but, above all, by mutual interest: one that demanded Britain see in her colonies the means to retain her commercial independence. The United States was challenging British supremacy and the only solution was to create a rival to American power. He attacked the "wild and destructive theories" of the free trade economists, arguing "There is no Friendship in Trade". Britain must hold to the tenets of the old commercial system upon which her commercial life depended. But there must be changes to meet the challenge of the United States. Enlarging on the free port idea, he recommended the establishment of free commercial cities in all the colonies, and particularly British North America, as entrepôts to draw in the productions of the world and allow the colonies to compete successfully with the Americans.

As in 1806, modifications to the old commercial system would not be sufficient in themselves. The very structure of colonial government would have to be changed by reuniting the Canadas and forming another government over the maritime colonies. The "miserable and contracted policy" of many petty governments had to be reversed or the whole would be inevitably overwhelmed by the vast increasing power of the United States. Britain must, before it was too late, create in the continent of North America a power to rival that of the United States in her own interest. If Britain was not prepared to do so, then it would be better, he suggested, for her "to surrender the whole by a friendly compact and Treaty" as it would not be worth defending possessions which, in their present state, were of small value and would be lost in a war with the United States. This note of despair became more pronounced in succeeding years, but it did not stop him from continuing to advocate the changes he believed so necessary to save British North America.

The re-opening of free ports encouraged Uniacke and his fellow Nova Scotians to believe that Britain was at last turning her attention to

---

39. Uniacke to Dalhousie, August 13, 1817, Board of Trade, 1, Vol. 136, P.R.O.

Nova Scotia. The Anglo-American Convention of 1818 shattered these hopes. The Convention re-opened the fisheries to the Americans upon terms only slightly less favourable than before the war — a war which Nova Scotians assumed had forever abrogated American fishing privileges. The Halifax Committee of Trade, angered by the betrayal, turned to the legislature for action, and in particular to Uniacke, who again took the initiative to organize a select committee of the council and the assembly to consider what steps were necessary to obtain a relaxation of restrictions on colonial trade.[40]

The result was a printed report of the council and assembly entitled *Proceedings of the General Assembly upon the Convention Concluded Between His Majesty and the United States of America.* This report was the most comprehensive and concerted attempt made by any British American colony up to that time to influence the British government to change its attitude toward the colonies. It not only concerned itself with Nova Scotian interests, but also with those of British America as a whole, and its proposals were designed to impress upon the British government the necessity for a fundamental change in colonial policy. It was written in the knowledge that there was a growing disenchantment in Britain with colonies. Uniacke was the main drafter and the report comes alive with his pungent language. It was the re-admittance of the Americans to the fishery that angered Nova Scotians the most, and "deprived us of this our last resource, and [has] left us almost without hope". Having given vent to this despair, the report turned to Uniacke's old theme, that the United States was as "enterprising a rival as she [Britain] ever had to contend with", and that Britain must "strengthen her Colonies in North America ... to enable them to stand by her side with effect, when the struggle for which the United States are so manifestly preparing shall take place".

In the past Uniacke had argued for the reuniting of the other maritime colonies to Nova Scotia as a matter of political necessity. The 1819 Report questioned the very legality of the "variety of dismemberments" since the separation of Prince Edward Island in 1769; Uniacke argued that the Crown, having established the boundaries and constitution of Nova Scotia in 1763, could not by any subsequent act change them.[41] It was a shrewd approach and may well

---

40. Motion by Uniacke in J.L.C., February 15, 1819.
41. Uniacke's argument was undoubtedly based on the 1774 judgement of Lord Mansfield of the Court of King's Bench in the case Campbell versus Hall in which he stated that once the prerogative power had been used to settle a new form of government on a colony, it would not be used again either to change the constitution or legislate for a colony. Judgement in Shortt and Doughty, *Documents Relating to the Constitutional History of Canada 1759-1828*, Vol. 1 (Ottawa, 1907) pp. 522-31.

have been a factor in the British government's decision to reunite Cape Breton to Nova Scotia. Certainly when the legality of the re-annexation was questioned, the legal adviser to the colonial office, James Stephens, argued that the original separation had been illegal.[42]

The report was not just a reiteration of colonial complaints, but a vigorous and enlightened critique of colonial policy. It was a reflection of a new energy that was pervading Nova Scotian life after 1815, a period of growing self-confidence and new ventures. D.C. Harvey has called this time "the intellectual awakening of Nova Scotia".[43] A new and energetic generation came to the fore, often rivals for office, but united in their Nova Scotianess, and too confident to need to believe, as their fathers had done, that Nova Scotia was somehow divinely favoured in a world awash with revolution. Unlike most of their fathers, also, they were native born, more secular and open to the liberalizing winds of change of the 19th century. Some, like Thomas Chandler Haliburton, became conservative with age, others such as Samuel Cunard found Nova Scotia too small for their commercial genius; still others, notably Joseph Howe, led their fellow Nova Scotians to the triumph of responsible government. Intellectually and politically the period from the War of 1812 to responsible government in 1848 was Nova Scotia's great age.

The new generation viewed Uniacke with some awe, as indeed did the general populace. When he and his six sons, all of whom were over six feet tall, walked through the streets of Halifax together, such walks were remembered by later generations as a grand and remarkable sight.[44] T.C. Haliburton dedicated his *General Description of Nova Scotia* to him, eulogizing him as "a Gentleman whose eloquence at the Bar, and extensive knowledge in the Legislature, are equalled by few, and excelled by none in America".[45] Young Nova Scotians who had trained in his office and were beginning to make their mark included Henry Cogswell, Lawrence O'Connor Doyle and his own son, James Boyle Uniacke, who became the first premier under responsible government.

He continued to entertain lavishly both at his town house and at the

---

42. James Stephen to Wilmot Horton, n.d. miscellaneous, CO 217, Vol. 143, P.R.O.

43. D.C. Harvey "The Intellectual Awakening of Nova Scotia", *Dalhousie Review*, Vol. 13, No. 1 (April 1933) pp. 1-22.

44. The tradition lasted into this century. See Constance Piers, "Mount Uniacke: An Old Colonial Mansion and Its Historic Heirlooms".

45. T.C. Haliburton, *A General Description of Nova Scotia* (Halifax, printed at the Royal Acadian School, 1823).

Mount, which, in the words of one contemporary, became almost like a "fashionable watering place".[46] His guests dined off the Wedgwood creamware banquetting service said to have been used by the Duchess of Richmond at her ball for the Duke of Wellington on the eve of Waterloo. Among the many guests was Lord Dalhousie; he had succeeded Sherbrooke in 1816.[47] Dalhousie's aide, Captain W. Hay, reminisced in later years how Uniacke would "assemble all his guests round a log fire in his smoking room each with his pipe or cigar and goodly supply of whisky and rum on the round table, and we were fully prepared for an evening's entertainments". Hay found Uniacke "one of the most clever, amusing and interesting persons that could be possibly imagined in any society, full of anecdotes, and knowing right well how to tell them".[48] Dalhousie himself thought Uniacke's stories generally inclined to the wonderful. After he had moved to Quebec as governor general, in 1820, Dalhousie carried on a full correspondence with Uniacke and other Nova Scotians, and on his return visit to Halifax in 1823, Uniacke was chosen to preside at a public dinner given in his honour.

Uniacke had a more intimate relationship with Dalhousie than with any other governor, with the possible exception of Parr. A governor of great energy with a somewhat exalted notion of the powers of the royal prerogative, Dalhousie lacked that firmness and wisdom that Sherbrooke had demonstrated or even the charm of his successor Sir James Kempt. But whatever his faults, Dalhousie made a greater effort than any other governor to shake Nova Scotians out of their economic lethargy. Much of his energy was directed to encouraging farmers to emulate the new farming techniques being used in Britain. In this he was ably supported by the publication of John Young's "Letters to Agricola" in the *Acadian Recorder* which inspired the formation of agricultural societies and a Central Board of Agriculture. Uniacke, already attempting to apply scientific farming methods on his own estate, became an enthusiastic supporter and wrote letters to Agricola describing his own agricultural experiments. When there was criticism of some of Young's advice, Uniacke in his inimitable style told him that "Few can expect to escape criticism in this age of Scepticism. Why

---

46. Mr. W.H. Hill, "Rambles among the Leaves from my Scrapbook" as quoted in L.G. Power, "Richard John Uniacke", p. 112.

47. On his travels about the province Dalhousie seems to have always stopped at the Mount for a visit. See Marjory Whitelaw, ed., *The Dalhousie Journals* (Oberon, c. 1978) which covers his time in Nova Scotia.

48. Captain W. Hay, C.B., *Reminiscences 1808-1815 under Wellington, Part II; Nova Scotia and Canada 1817-1823 with the Earl of Dalhousie* (London, 1901) p. 272.

should Agricola repine, when he sees that even our own blessed saviour was publickly reviled by a combination of impious infidels".[49]

In his many travels about the province Dalhousie was shocked at the thousands of acres held by speculative land owners and retarding the advancement of settlement. Under Prevost and Sherbrooke there had been some escheating, but Dalhousie pursued the matter with more vigor. During Uniacke's visit to England in 1806 he had convinced the British government to allow the free granting of land once again. He impressed upon Dalhousie the injustice of speculators holding extensive tracts of land without any intention of improving them or bringing in settlers.[50] He had done most of the legal work of escheating of lands for the settlement of the loyalists and was very familiar with the legal problems involved. As he told Dalhousie he had drafted the regulations so that the governor could enforce the terms and conditions against speculators in large tracts of land. With Dalhousie's backing the escheat process was quickened; Uniacke as attorney general supervised the legal work, and between 1819 and 1821 nearly 100,000 acres were reclaimed by the government. This was one means of opening the wilderness to settlers. Another way was a programme of planned settlement.

Uniacke wanted Dalhousie to use the rapidly forming agricultural societies to obtain information on what lands were available for settlement in each district. These lands would then be surveyed and laid out in sections, with the societies' committees made responsible for putting new settlers on the lands. In addition, the societies would be responsible for determining the numbers and types of tradesmen and labourers required. Uniacke's proposal went as far as issuing tickets to immigrants, allowing them lodging en route to their alloted destination, and printing advertisements in Britain listing the opportunities for employment and settlement in Nova Scotia. This was to prevent the province from being "inundated ... by a wretched description of people who have expended their last shilling nay even their wearing apparel in endeavouring to procure a passage to this country peruaded by the artful crimps in the shipping engaged in the timber trade, that this is the most convenient and contiguous road to the Ohio or Illinois".[51] A letter from a "Friendless Emigrant" in the *Acadian Recorder* provided a graphic illustration of the evils of which Uniacke complained; the writer described how immigrants who wanted to engage in farming finally gave it up "when they learned the difficulties

---

49. Uniacke to Agricola (John Young) February 29, 1820, RG 8, Vol. 2, P.A.N.S.
50. Uniacke to Dalhousie, January 26, 1819, RG 1, Vol. 306, No. 39, P.A.N.S.
51. Ibid.

Mount Uniacke   John Elliott Woolford c. 1817

The dining room at Mount Uniacke

The library at Mount Uniacke

Cover:
The Hon. Richard John Uniacke (1753-1830)
Portrait by Robert Field
Collection: Nova Scotia Museum, at Mount Uniacke

Richard John Uniacke Jr. (1789-1834)
Son of The Hon. Richard John Uniacke
Watercolor on Ivory
Collection: Nova Scotia Museum, at Mount Uniacke

Crest and Bookplate

Alicia Uniacke (1787-1841)
Third daughter of Richard John Uniacke
Portrait by Robert Field
Collection: Nova Scotia Museum, at Mount Uniacke

Chief Justice Sampson S. Blowers
(1742-1842)
By John Poad Drake 1820

Governor Sir John Wentworth, Bart.
(1737-1820)
Portrait by Robert Field
Oil on Canvas c. 1808
Collection of Government House
Province of Nova Scotia

attending it; their pockets... completely drained... by interested speculators...".[52]

By 1819, when Uniacke put forward his proposals, the post-Napoleonic wave of immigration was well underway. This wave brought 40,000 immigrants to Nova Scotia and, combined with natural growth, increased the population from 75,000 in 1815 to 200,000 by 1838. Immediately after the war Nova Scotians had been interested in attracting immigration, and the address to the Prince Regent in 1814 recommended that bounties be offered to immigrants. Uniacke's idea of using the agricultural societies to assist immigrants probably had its origin in an earlier proposal made in the assembly. Action, however, was not taken until after Uniacke submitted his own ideas.

The Central Board of Agriculture, incorporated in 1819 and supported by public funds, was instructed to seek information on the prospects for settlement and employment in the districts. Nova Scotians wishing to sell their farms or needing labour were encouraged to make known their requirements to the board. In 1821 boards of land commissioners were set up in the districts to assist settlement and discourage speculation. Uniacke's proposals had been to use the voluntary efforts of the agricultural societies, but the system adopted did not differ in concept from that which he had advocated.

Adam Smith's *An Inquiry into the Nature and Causes of the Wealth of Nations* became popular during Dalhousie's governship. Joseph Howe remarked in one of his reminiscences that "Every fellow who wanted an office or wished to get an invitation to Government House... talked of Adam Smith".[53] Uniacke may well have read Smith before Dalhousie's arrival, and from him derived his ideas on the importance of the accumulation of capital and the establishment of banks for the profitable employment of surplus capital. The post-war depression and crop failures had placed credit at so low an ebb that the best landed security would not allow the farmer to obtain capital for improvements. The "dreadful extortions", he told Dalhousie, that settlers had to submit to obtain even a cow or sheep through "channels of polluted extortion", were a disgrace in a province where "liberal principles" usually prevailed.[54] Only by the establishment of banks that would loan money on the security of land could the conditions of the farmer be improved. The use of all surplus capital had to be preserved for the use

---

52. *Acadian Recorder*, April 25, 1818.

53. Joseph Howe, "Notes on Several Governors and their Influence, *Collections* N.S.H.S., Vol. 17, p. 197.

54. Uniacke to Dalhousie, January 25, 1819, RG 1, Vol. 306, No. 38, P.A.N.S.

of Nova Scotians, and to achieve this the course adopted in other countries should be followed of enabling the owners of surplus capital to invest advantageously in Nova Scotia.

There was, however, much opposition to banks particularly in the country districts where treasury notes supplemented barter as the main medium of exchange. In 1812 Nova Scotia had begun to issue treasury notes as legal tender to serve as a currency, specie being continuously drained out of the province by the adverse balance of trade, and further issues of notes brought the total circulation up to £40,000 by 1819.[55]

There had been attempts in 1801 and 1811 to gain assembly approval for the incorporation of a bank, but the proposers wanted a monopoly, and the assembly would not grant this. In 1819, Henry Cogswell presented a bill in the assembly for the creation of a joint stock public bank to be called the Halifax Bank Company, its board of directors to be responsible to a supervisory board made up of the council and fourteen members of the assembly. The assembly was reluctant, because many country members were more concerned with the establishment of loan offices throughout the province and with the justifiable fear that the more secure bank notes would cause the provincial treasury notes to depreciate. The council was prepared to accept loan offices for Kings and Annapolis counties only, but refused to accept changes which the assembly made to the bank bill that would not have allowed bank notes to be legal tender; consequently, Cogswell's bank bill failed to pass.

After the council refused to agree to loan offices throughout the province, some merchants announced their intention to seek approval for the Halifax Bank Company. Uniacke entered the debate publicly with a letter to the *Halifax Journal*.[56] Uniacke was familiar with the 1810 British Parliamentary Committee Report on the High Prices of Bullion, and cited it, as well as Adam Smith, in elucidating the differences between value in use and value in exchange and the character of money. Money was a "creature of human imagination", but whatever was used as money had to have an intrinsic value, and prices became higher or lower according to the availability of specie or any other article used as money. This premise provided the basis of his argument against the wish of the Halifax merchants to raise the value in Halifax currency of the Spanish gold doubloon from £3 17s 6d to £4, with the hope of stopping the constant drain of specie. But Uniacke was at a loss to

---

55. See J.S. Martell, *A Documentary Study of Provincial Finance and Currency 1812-36* (Public Archives of Nova Scotia, 1941).

56. *The Halifax Journal*, March 22, 1819.

explain how raising the nominal value would stop the exportation of specie; the intrinsic value would remain the same, unless changed by supply and demand, and this would be reflected in the rate of exchange with other countries. The measure by the merchants failed and simply depreciated the provincial notes in circulation.

The Halifax merchants wanted more specie to facilitate trading, while the farmers, tradesmen and country merchants wanted more paper money issued to increase the amount in circulation and to pay for roads and other desired expenditures. Uniacke did not consider there was a shortage of specie, or a need to increase the amount in circulation, although he had no apprehension of a provincial debt if the money was borrowed with interest and not found by issuing of a paper currency. His answer was the establishment of a publicly incorporated provincial bank modeled upon the Royal Bank of Scotland, which was a joint stock bank paying interest on deposits and lending money to the enterprising. This would draw into circulation the large accumulated capital of the province, which he estimated was £120,000 in hoarded specie. This specie would be used for foreign exchange, and paper bank notes for domestic circulation.

He drew a sharp distinction between paper currency issued by government and by a public bank. The issue of paper currency issued by a government was a form of forced loan destined to depreciate, but that issued by a bank was regulated by the amount of specie on deposit. A major advantage would be that bills drawn on England would be remitted through the bank to a bank in London, which would then provide credit for use by Nova Scotian merchants anywhere in the world; thus no one would want to export specie when the bank, through its credit arrangements, would be able to provide it anywhere.

Proposals for a bank were again submitted to council in 1822. Uniacke and his son, Richard John, were listed as subscribers for an incorporated bank with a monopoly for twenty-one years, unless a provincial bank was established. Nothing came of this proposal, but in 1824 Uniacke was asked by Governor Sir James Kempt to draft regulations for a savings bank; there was opposition in the council, however, and there the proposal died. Although his draft regulations are not extant, it is clear he wanted a provincial bank that would be a "creature of the Legislature" with sole right to issue notes as legal tender.[57] These bank notes would then replace the issues of government treasury notes. The government, when it wanted money,

---

57. This is what he had proposed in his letter to *The Halifax Journal* and there is no reason to believe he had changed his mind.

would borrow from the bank, making arrangements to pay the interest and sink the principal. By this means the provincial credit would be maintained and confidence engendered. He most likely did not believe that government funds should be used to support a provincial bank, as was the case with the Bank of Upper Canada incorporated in 1821. The mercantile members of the council presumably wanted to avoid any direct government control over the operations of a bank or even to have a provincial bank with a monopoly on the issuing of notes, hence the opposition to Uniacke's draft.

Another proposal for a bank was made in 1825, and this made no reference to councillors or assemblymen having a supervisory role. It was defeated in the assembly by the county members, who feared the possible depreciation of provincial treasury notes. The result was the establishment in the same year of the Halifax Banking Company, a private bank, known commonly as "Collins' Bank", over which the assembly had no control. Not until 1832, two years after Uniacke's death, did Nova Scotia have an incorporated bank with the establishment of the Bank of Nova Scotia. Uniacke's fears that large issues of government paper money would lead to depreciation and debt were fully justified: in 1834 the assembly legislated that all banks, firms and individuals had to redeem their notes in specie, to stop further depreciation, but the treasury notes were allowed to find their own level; the result was a financial crash.

While busy proferring advice to governors and to the general public, Uniacke did not neglect the interests of his sons. Having established Richard John in Cape Breton with the hope he would soon become chief justice, he set his sights upon the judgeship of the Vice Admiralty Court and a council seat for Crofton. The contrast between the two sons could not have been greater, although both had the natural eloquence so characteristic of all the Uniackes: Richard John, unmarried and considered the handsomest man in Halifax, had more of his father's wit but less of his drive and ability. His outgoing character and charm sufficed for most to overlook his vanity and inherited temper. A favourite of Dalhousie's, he was praised by him at one Charitable Irish Society dinner "in terms so flattering that... it touched the heart of every person" present.[58]

Crofton had none of his younger brother's charm but the same inherited haughtiness. In ability he was superior, but he never achieved the success he and his father believed his due. In 1815 he became surrogate to Judge Alexander Croke who retired the next year, at which

58. Minutes of the Charitable Irish Society, March 17, 1819, MG 20, Vol. 66, P.A.N.S.

time it was presumed that the appointment would go to Crofton. However, Sherbrooke demurred making the appointment because he believed that Crofton would also automatically become a member of the council and would rank only behind the chief justice and the bishop. As neither could become administrator in the absence of the governor, it was quite conceivable that Crofton could assume that position. In precedent-conscious Nova Scotia this was unacceptable, and Sherbrooke temporarily appointed Michael Wallace, a merchant and the provincial treasurer, to keep the peace.

Undaunted, Uniacke prevailed upon Lord Shannon to procure an interview for Crofton at the Colonial Office and wrote directly to the Secretary of State for the Colonies, Lord Bathurst. Arguing that the position required a legal background, which Wallace did not have, Uniacke then launched into a tirade against the loyalists, blaming them for all the trouble in Nova Scotia. He told Bathurst that he had often defeated their "artful projects", and was thus hated "from one end of the United States to another". The Nova Scotian loyalists, notwithstanding all their professions of loyalty, "were the most malignant enemies of Great Britain", and they had done him "many injuries and now transfer their hatred to my sons".[59] While claiming that Crofton had not expected the appointment or a seat on the council, Uniacke nevertheless solicited both an interview and the appointment for him. He referred Bathurst to his services to the Crown and to his Irish patrons, rhetorically asking him what encouragement could there be for fathers to well educate their children, if a merchant was competent to sit as a judge.

Crofton delivered his father's letter to Bathurst, but was told that the appointment was vested in the Lords Commissioners of the Admiralty. There he secured the appointment and support for a council seat. Upon his return to Nova Scotia in 1817, he found the opposition to his having a seat just as strong as before. Dalhousie, now the governor, asked the council for an opinion on Crofton's right to a seat and the council voted six to four against. Uniacke was supported by Charles Hill, Charles Morris, and Thomas Jeffery, two of whom were related to him through marriages of his children; Crofton himself had married Dorothea Fawson, the niece of Charles Morris. Dalhousie was determined not to allow Crofton to have a council seat, because it was a

---

59. Uniacke to Bathurst, May 4, 1816, miscellaneous, CO 217, Vol. 98, P.R.O. Henry Goulbourn replied on behalf of Bathurst assuring Uniacke that Sherbrooke's refusal to appoint Crofton "was not entered into . . . to diminish the consideration to which from the length and importance of those services you are so justly entitled", July 6, 1816, CO 218, Vol. 29, P.R.O.

matter "likely to affect that distinction in our society, which had hitherto attached to the members of His Majesty's Council". That private quarrels of considerable bitterness were at the root of the dispute was clear to Dalhousie and, as he told Bathurst, he was actuated by no personal feelings towards Crofton, "nor by any participation, the most distant in private quarrels".[60] To make matters worse, Crofton insulted Dalhousie in a letter asking for a subscription on behalf of the immigrant poor, whereupon he wrote Uniacke that Crofton was not to visit Government House again, nor would he recommend him for a council seat.

Having gone to such efforts to secure the appointment, Crofton resigned after two years and went to practise law in England. With peace the judgeship was less lucrative and there had been criticism of his judgements. Probably the dislike he had engendered was also a factor in his decision, one which his father did not approve. He wanted his sons in Nova Scotia, but Nova Scotia was too small for all the Uniackes to have the offices their father wanted for them.

Meanwhile Richard John had failed to secure the chief justiceship of Cape Breton, even after interventions at the Colonial Office by his father and Crofton. He returned to Halifax, which was socially more congenial to him, and succeeded his father as advocate general of the Vice Admiralty Court.

It was Richard John who fought at the last fatal duel on record in Nova Scotia. In the early hours of July 21, 1819 he killed the merchant William Bowie. During a suit in the Supreme Court, young Uniacke probably had suggested Bowie was engaged in smuggling. Whatever his remarks, Bowie took great exception to them and in a letter cast aspersions on Uniacke's honour as a gentleman. When he refused to retract them, Uniacke challenged. Uniacke's second was an Edward M'Sweney who had been involved in duels before and was also indebted to Bowie. It was M'Sweney who insisted the duelists fire a second time after neither had been hit during the first exchange. The duel and death of Bowie shocked Halifax; the flags of all the vessels in the harbour were hung at half mast, and a "general gloom seemed to pervade all ranks of society".[61] The drama of his trial for murder was captured by the *Acadian Recorder:*

> ... about 20 minutes past 11 o'clock, the Hon. Richard J. Uniacke entered the Court, supporting his son on his right arm... He advanced to the Bench and stated to the Court, under feeling which evidently almost overpowered him, that he had an

---

60. Dalhousie to Bathurst, November 11, 1817, CO 217, Vol. 97, P.R.O.
61. *Acadian Recorder*, July 24, 1819.

important and melancholy duty to perform that whatever his feelings might be upon the occasion, they must be subservient to the laws of the land, which he did not doubt would be administered with justice and mercy.[62]

Uniacke, with his fine white locks falling over his herculean shoulders, carrying a big ivory-headed cane and wearing an eye glass remained in court during the trial. Norman, his eldest son, sat at the court table with S.G.W. Archibald, the King's Counsel. Crofton remained at Richard John's side throughout the trial. Messieurs Chipman, Hill, Nutting, Fraser, and Fairbanks, all gentlemen of the bar, spoke in young Uniacke's favour. His own and the honour of his family was his only defence, and, as was expected, he was found not guilty. Uniacke, as attorney general, should have prosecuted the case, but could not, and Robie, the solicitor general, refused on grounds on his friendship for Bowie. The onus fell on S.G.W. Archibald, and Uniacke had always a great regard for him because of his role in "Dick's unfortunate affair", as he called it.[63] Dick, if he had been found guilty, would probably not have been hanged, although in England in 1808 a Major Campbell had been executed for a similar offence. His most likely punishment would have been the branding of his left thumb with the letter "M" for murderer.

62. *Ibid.*, July 31, 1819.
63. Uniacke to his son James Boyle, April 3, 1824, MG 1, Vol. 926, P.A.N.S.

Chapter Five

It is Likely Hostile Influence Will Be Employed

In his latter day determination to preserve the Church of England as the established church of Nova Scotia, Uniacke was responsible for much of the religious bitterness that engulfed Nova Scotia in the first decades of the 19th century. His attitude to religion had moved from his early anti-clericalism to the fervour of a convert, but his conversion was more political than religious. He could support the cause of Catholic emancipation and at the same time use his position as principal law officer and member of council to resist the attempts by those Protestants who dissented from the Church of England to gain religious and educational equality. The exclusion of non-Anglicans from King's College after 1803 by requiring subscription to the Thirty-nine Articles ended the religious harmony that had prevailed in Nova Scotia. Led by Uniacke and Bishop John Inglis, high church Anglicans were able to stop the Reverend Thomas McCulloch from establishing a college at Pictou open to all denominations. More than any other action by high church Anglicans, Uniacke's opposition changed what had been religious controversies into hard-fought political issues.

In the Ireland of Uniacke's youth the Church of England had all the vices that beset Anglicanism in the Hanoverian age and almost none of its virtues.[1] It was the established church, but its membership was confined to adherents of the Protestant Ascendancy in the southern counties. In the north, Presbyterians were dominant, but were excluded from public office as Dissenters.

Roman Catholics, whose religion was proscribed, were the majority in Ireland. An underground church had survived, and by the time of Uniacke's birth priests openly ministered to their flocks. It was one such priest who had so influenced Uniacke as a boy that his father had

---

1. For the vices and virtues of 18th Century Anglicanism see Rev. Norman Sykes. *Church and States in England in the XVIIIth Century,* reprint (Octagon Books, New York, 1975).

feared he might be converted. To the youngest son of a prosperous family who could not expect to succeed to his father's estate, the ministry of the established church had its attractions. Under the influence of a grandmother he had inclined to a religious life, but had become "so disgusted with the Hyprocrisy and selfish rapacity" of the ministers of the established church that he had formed "an early antipathy" to the church.[2] Even when in later years he had become a staunch supporter of the Church of England, he wrote to his youngest son, whom he was encouraging to enter the ministry, of the "insatiable rapacity" of many bishops and clergy. This estrangement from the church of his upbringing continued in the New World.

Upon his return to Nova Scotia after completing his legal studies in Ireland, Uniacke had every reason to adhere to the established church. As solicitor general he was probably the only official who did not. Even leading Dissenters and Catholics paid pew rents at St. Paul's to display their loyalty to the British connection and acceptance of the Church of England as the established church. An act of the Nova Scotian assembly in 1758 had declared the Church of England the established church, but it had also provided for "liberty of conscience" for dissenting Protestants.[3] Anglicans were a minority and even after the settlement of the loyalists never made up more than a quarter of the population. Dissenters of various persuasions were very much in the majority. Nonetheless, for those ambitious for office adherence to the established church was a distinct advantage. Uniacke knew this but nevertheless chose to become a member of the Protestant Dissenting Church.

He joined at a time when this church was shifting from New England Congregationalism to Scottish Presbyterianism. This change was formalized by the appointment of the Rev. Andrew Brown as minister in 1787. Brown was of the established Church of Scotland, which outside Scotland was often accepted in practice as having status equal to the Church of England.

By selecting Brown as their minister Halifax Dissenters deliberately made a political rather than a religious choice. Part of Brown's salary came from the Nova Scotian civil list and Anglicans viewed his appointment favourably. Leaders of the two churches were united in

---

2. Uniacke to his son Andrew, January 10, 1828, Vertical Manuscript File: Uniacke, Richard John Uniacke, Letters to Andrew Mitchell Uniacke.

3. The extent to which the Church of England in law was the established church in Nova Scotia is examined in Nora Story, "The Churches and the State in Nova Scotia, 1749-1840: An Outline of Problems and Policy", unpublished manuscript, library of P.A.N.S.

their antipathy to Dissenters of all descriptions and particularly Secessionist Presbyterians.[4]

For one of Uniacke's position and class not to have belonged to a church would have been unheard of in Nova Scotia. The Protestant Dissenting Church served Protestants who were not Anglicans, drawing its membership from many countries and denominations.[5] It seems to have had a vitality that was lacking at St. Paul's and this, with his antipathy to the Church of England, probably attracted Uniacke. He never became an elder but in 1785 was on the committee selected to find a successor to Brown.[6] While waiting for his successor, Uniacke was made chairman of the committee chosen to request the Anglican Rev. George Wright to minister to the congregation. Even as a member of the Dissenting Church, he had his children baptised at St. Paul's. This was not uncommon practice, but does suggest his distaste for the Church of England was lessening, particularly as he does not seem to have had his three eldest children, born between 1777 to 1783, baptised at all.

He did not pay pew rents at St. Paul's until 1801, when he severed all connections with the Dissenting Church.[7] Just why he did so at this time is not clear. There is no evidence of any quarrel within the church. He had already been appointed attorney general and adherence to the Church of Scotland was no bar to preferment. Three years earlier he had told his son Norman that he should content himself with the forms of religion as by law established in England or Scotland. Either system was good, in his opinion, and marked the wisdom of the people who planned it. If he had had in his youth an irreligious period, he was now fully convinced of the truth of Christian doctrine; it was that of the 18th century Anglicanism, moderate, reasonable and temperate, but under siege from religious enthusiasts and rational disbelievers. It was the

---

4. The first secession from the established Church of Scotland was in 1733 and over the authority for appointing ministers to churches. The Secessionists themselves divided in 1745-7 over the refusal of the "anti-burghers" to take an oath that implied recognition of the Church of Scotland as the "true religion". Most of the early Presbyterian ministers in Nova Scotia were from the Secessionist churches although many, if not the majority of Scots in Nova Scotia, were adherents of the Church of Scotland.

5. The Protestant Dissenting Church was renamed St. Matthew's in 1815 and for a history of this church see W.C. Murray, "History of St. Matthew's Church", *Collections*, N.S.H.S., Vol. XVI, pp. 137-70, and Rev. George Patterson's Papers, MG 1, Vol. 742, Folder II, St. Matthew's Church, P.A.N.S.

6. Uniacke's activities in the Protestant Dissenting Church are taken from the records of church in MG 4, Vol. 55, P.A.N.S.

7. The lists of pewholders for St. Paul's, 1798-1816, are in RG 1, Vol. 433, Nos. 118-121, P.A.N.S.

latter Uniacke most detested; "the Irreligious and Desolute who vainly wish to believe that there is no God". They were "wretches" whose "very breath carries with it the seeds of Contention and their Abode is the Habitation of filth and Corruption". His advice to Norman was to shun these "vipers" and be a "Modest Religious man" who would find the discharge of his religious duties attended with pleasure and would open his mind to "scenes of future existence far beyond the present life".[8]

It was not a religious conversion that drew Uniacke back into the church of his birth, but a conservatism which deepened as he saw Christian society threatened by the evil principles emanating from the French Revolution. He had come to accept that if religion were destroyed, so would government be. An established church which would inculcate morality and loyalty had become a necessity for him if the British constitution were to survive and not be overborne by the heresies of republicanism, atheism and democracy. His earlier antipathy vanished as he came to share the prevailing conservatism and Erastianism of the Church of England. Erastianism viewed the church as the handmaiden of the state; for Uniacke the established church was a mainstay of the British constitution and bulwark against revolutionary ideas. It is most remarkable and probably a comment on the respect, and perhaps the fear, in which he was held, that there is no evidence that his conversion was ever thrown back at him during the bitter church and state quarrels that so divided Nova Scotians after 1813.

One of the prejudices of his age that Uniacke did not share was the intolerance toward Catholics so engrained in Protestantism. No Protestant did more for Catholic emancipation in Nova Scotia than he. During his return to Ireland to complete his legal studies, parliament had passed an act in 1778 repealing some of the more vicious penalties and disabilities against English Catholics. He had been present in Dublin for the great debate over the second Irish Catholic Act passed the same year. Once back in Nova Scotia and a member of the assembly, he took up the cause of Catholic relief. An assembly act of 1758 had virtually proscribed the Catholic religion. However the need to reconcile the Indians and returning Acadians to British rule, and a generally more tolerant feeling led to the passage of an act in 1782 repealing many of the provisions of the 1758 act.

The act was disallowed by the British government because it departed too much from the parliamentary act of 1778. The following year Uniacke redrafted the act to conform to the British one, and this

---

8. Uniacke to his son Norman, November 1, MG 1, Vol. 926, No. 99.

was passed and confirmed by the British government.[9] This new act allowed Catholics to acquire land, build churches and have their own priests, provided they took the prescribed oath. In 1786 Uniacke drafted another statute allowing Catholics to establish schools, and three years later they were granted the franchise. These acts were repaid by an unquestioned loyalty to the British connection, well personified by the Rev. Edmund Burke, who became Vicar General in Halifax in 1801. An Irish priest, Burke was one of the most colourful, dynamic and intellectually able men of this period in Nova Scotia, but he was also one of the most disputatious.

In 1802 Burke petitioned for the incorporation of himself, the Roman Catholic Bishop of Quebec and others of the Quebec hierarchy to enable them to receive donations and erect schools.[10] Burke was not only requesting a licence to erect a school, he was also asking for legal recognition of the Catholic hierarchy in Nova Scotia. The principal reason the 1782 relief act had been disallowed was that it implied the establishment in law of the Roman Catholic religion in Nova Scotia.[11] There was no objection to the principle of toleration, but any recognition in law of a Catholic hierarchy was unacceptable. No one was more aware of the legal implications of Burke's petition than Uniacke, who had redrafted the 1782 act. Wentworth, as governor, refused to issue any licence and referred the matter to London. He also sent Uniacke as attorney general and as a personal friend of Burke to inform Burke of his refusal. Burke simply ignored the refusal and started a school anyway, for which he received a licence in 1806.

In the intervening period he became the main disputant in what the Roman Catholic Bishop of Newfoundland called Burke's denominational "Paper War".[12] The Catholic hierarchy was opposed to Burke's disputatious activities, but he ignored them as he did others. In his charge delivered to his clergy in 1803 Bishop Inglis blamed the teachings of the French Catholic church for the republican and atheistic doctrines of the French Revolution. Inglis was not anti-Catholic, but he

9. Uniacke stated he was responsible in Appendix II, *The Attorney General's Answer*, Halifax, February 16, 1804, p. 51 to *A Charge Delivered to the Clergy of the Diocesess (sic) of Nova Scotia at the Triennial Visitation holden in the months of June and August, 1803 by the Right Reverend Charles Inglis DD*, second edition, Halifax, 1804 (hereafter *The Attorney General's Answer*).

10. The petition is in RG 1, Vol. 303, No. 3.

11. Unsigned to Lord President (Committee of the Privy Council), May 12, 1783, CO 217, Vol. 35, P.R.O.

12. For the "Paper War", see Leonora A. Merrigan, "The Life and Times of Edmund Burke in Nova Scotia 1801-1820" (unpublished M.A. thesis, Saint Mary's University, Halifax, 1971) pp. 20-40.

was opposed to Burke's school because he feared that Burke intended to turn it into a seminary. Burke read Inglis' charge when he had just finished writing a *Letter of Instruction to the Catholic Missionaries of Nova Scotia and Its Dependencies*, and he immediately attached a postcript attacking Inglis in very satiric language for his opposition to his school and his anti-Catholic statements.

Copies of the letter and postcript were sent by Burke to Wentworth, Uniacke and others. Uniacke was horrified and in his published reply lectured Burke on the consequences of stirring up "animosities" between Protestants and Roman Catholics. Burke's letter had been addressed by order of the Bishop of Quebec and had been published by Burke as Vicar General of Nova Scotia, and it was this that most disturbed Uniacke. He informed Burke in the clearest language that the privileges of Catholics solely depended on the 1783 and 1786 acts, and that there could be no question of establishing a Catholic hierarchy in Nova Scotia. The law was emphatic that whoever officiated as a Catholic priest did so by the choice of his congregation; Uniacke wanted to hear "no more of Bishops, Vicars General, or Missionaries in this Province, unless they are especially appointed by the King for that purpose". He recommended that Burke should unite with other Christians "to put down Atheism, Infidelity, Superstition and Idolatry, to which may be traced all the evils, that for some time past, have desolated Europe, and shaken civil and religious Society to its foundation".[13]

The "Paper War" begun by Burke did not subside until his death in 1820. Its only redeeming feature was the remarkably high level of scholarship displayed by Burke and the Secessionist minister at Pictou, Thomas McCulloch, the founder and principal of Pictou Academy; the latter entered the controversy later at the behest of the Anglicans, who found themselves in need of McCulloch's learning to defend the Protestant cause.

The need for an academy was sorely felt in Nova Scotia. No one knew it more than Uniacke, as the father of numerous sons, and no doubt he had them very much in mind when he moved the resolution in the 1787 session that led to the establishment of an academy at Windsor.[14] The academy was opened the next year with a grant from the assembly and in 1789 King's College was established with a

---

13. *The Attorney General's Answer*, pp. 53, 52 and 54.

14. *J.L.A.* November 13 and 19, 1787. In the 1790 assembly session Uniacke remarked that a child could be boarded and educated at the Academy for £20 per year, while the province paid eight or nine pounds more to maintain a vagabond, Beamish Murdoch, *History of Nova Scotia*, Vol. III, p. 82.

permanent annual grant of £400. The British government, for imperial reasons and those of church and state, supported the efforts to found a college. In 1790 royal approval was given for the institution, £1000 for its construction, and lands for an endowment as well as a royal charter were promised. The war with France intervened but the college managed to continue in operation. Uniacke, as speaker of the assembly, was named one of the governors, and as a member of the Protestant Dissenting Church, he was the only non-Anglican on the board. The Rev. William Cochran ran both the academy and the college and about 200 students, including Dissenters, passed through it until 1802, when the royal charter was granted. The charter ensured that King's would be under Anglican control, but it was the statutes drafted by the Board of Governors that decided whether King's would be open to Dissenters or exclusively an Anglican college.

Judge Alexander Croke, Chief Justice Blowers and Bishop Charles Inglis were chosen as a committee to draft the statutes. Croke and Blowers, both anti-clerical, contrived to exclude Bishop Inglis from participation in the drafting.[15] The statutes were modelled upon those of Oxford University and included provisions requiring students to subscribe to the Thirty-nine Articles upon entrance, as well as prohibiting students from attending any Dissenting church or meeting. The governors met for two weeks in July 1803 to consider the statutes.[16] Croke claimed that they were unanimously approved, but that later the bishop moved that the statutes requiring subscriptions to the Thirty-nine articles be revoked. His motion was defeated by a majority.[17] Those opposed were probably the bishop, Uniacke and James Stewart who had been educated at Edinburgh University where no religious tests were required. The statutes were printed and a copy sent to the Archbishop of Canterbury for approval. Inglis protested directly to the archbishop although he made no mention of statutes excluding Dissenters.[18] The illness and death of the archbishop delayed matters until Uniacke took up the question with his successor during

---

15. For Inglis' resentment at what he considered the anti-clericalism of the other two see Judith Fingard, *The Anglican Design in Loyalist Nova Scotia* 1783-1816 (S.P.C.K., London, 1972) pp. 152-3.

16. The minutes of the Board of Governors of King's College (hereafter B.G.K.C.) July 4-16 and 18, 1803, King's College Library, Halifax, N.S.

17. Protest by Judge Croke, Minutes, B.G.K.C., May 2, 1807. Wentworth, who with his cousin B. Wentworth were members of the board, obliquely suggests that the board was divided over the question. Wentworth to Scrope Bernard, October 12, 1806, RG 1, Vol. 54, pp. 120.

18. See Judith Fingard, *The Anglican Design in Nova Scotia*, p. 152.

his visit to England in 1806. Whether he did this with the authority of the other governors is not known, but he had at least one interview with the archbishop. As a result the archbishop sent Uniacke a note signifying his disapproval of the statutes until he had time to suggest alterations.[19] These he discussed with Prime Minister Lord Grenville and William Windham. Just before Uniacke's return to Nova Scotia, the archbishop sent him the alterations he wished adopted by the governors; the most important of these was that students would not be required to subscribe to the Thirty-nine Articles until graduation.[20] In practice this would allow Dissenters to obtain their education but not a degree, as was the case at Cambridge University. Uniacke must have been instrumental in securing this alteration in his interviews with the archbishop and Windham.

The governors accepted all the alterations with one minor exception. However, the revised statutes were never published, and it was the old statutes that governed entrance to King's. The exclusion of Dissenters from King's was a blow from which it and higher education in Nova Scotia has never fully recovered. Dissenters were prepared to accept Anglican control, if only because the British government was granting substantial financial aid, but refused to allow their sons to become apostates.

It was most likely Croke, supported by Blowers, who was able to nullify the crucial alteration. Both Croke and Inglis wrote the archbishop, Inglis supportive of the alteration and Croke in protest. In his protest Croke charged that abrogation of the statutes requiring subscription upon entrance would destroy all distinctions between the established church and those religions that were only tolerated by law, and would perpetuate dissent.[21] While in the first decade of the 19th century Uniacke would not accept Croke's exclusivist views and used his influence to resist them, in the next decade he came to embrace them with a vengeance.

Nova Scotians, although dismayed by the exclusivist character of King's, were more disturbed by the lack of primary and grammar school education. This was in part a reflection of the growing interest in England for the education of poor children. There the Bell and Lancastrian systems were being advocated, both of which used older children to instruct younger ones. The Lancastrian schools restricted

---

19. Archbishop Charles Manners Sutton to Uniacke, July 20, 1806, Papers relating to King's College, King's College Library.

20. Ibid., September 8, 1806 With the letter are the proposed alterations.

21. Protest by Judge Croke, Minutes, 2 May 1807, B.G.K.C.

denominational instruction to the home and church, whereas Anglican church schools used the Bell sstem.

In England latitudinarian or low church Anglicans and Methodists supported the Lancastrian system and high churchmen the Bell system. This split in support was reflected in Nova Scotia when Walter Bromley, of Methodist leanings, proposed in 1813 to establish a school modelled on the monitorial system, but with non-denominational religious instruction included in the curriculum. The Royal Acadian Society was established to support such a school to be named the Royal Acadian School, and a committee appointed to raise and expend funds. Ecumenical in composition, the committee included such prominent people as Governor Sir John Sherbrooke, and at the top of the list was Uniacke's name. From the beginning Judge Alexander Croke opposed the school because the children would not be instructed in Anglican doctrine. There then began a much heated "letters to the editor" debate, involving Croke, Bromley and Thomas McCulloch. The issue was further complicated by the formation of a branch of the British and Foreign Bible Society, which was evangelical and interdenominational. John Inglis, the son of Bishop Charles, opposed its formation, again reflecting the opposition to it in England by high churchmen. Many supporters of the Royal Acadian Society also became members of the British and Foreign Bible Society, creating further animosities among Anglicans as well as between Anglicans and Dissenters.

Croke had been invited to become vice president of the Royal Anglican Society but had refused. In a lengthy letter to the *Acadian Recorder* he argued for the teaching of the Anglican catechism in the school because Anglicanism was the religion that was established by law as the national religion.[22] Bromley retorted with an insulting diatribe which was replied to in kind. Thomas McCulloch entered the fray with a telling critique of Croke's arguments for control of education by the Church of England. Croke and McCulloch continued the controversy in a series of letters, and others joined the war of words with alacrity. Anglicans divided, some supporting the Royal Acadian School, while others saw it as "an artful design to undermine the Church of England and to promote the views of different sectaries".[23]

The latter group coalesced to form an extreme wing of the church and state party with its support concentrated in the council.[24] They

---

22. *Acadian Recorder*, August 14, 1813.
23. "Vox Clamantis", *Acadian Recorder*, September 11, 1813. In the same issue McCulloch did a masterful critique of Croke's letter of August 14.
24. See Nora Story "The Church and State Party in Nova Scotia, 1749-1851", *Collections*. N.S.H.S., Vol. 27. pp. 33-57.

were determined to uphold the privileges of the Church of England as the established church, however impolitic it might be in a society where its membership was a minority. Because in their minds church and state were inseparable, an attack on the established church was an attack on the British constitution. In a reflection of the philosophy of high church Tories in England hostility to the Church of England was interpreted as disloyal and revolutionary. Insinuations were made of disloyalty and republicanism against Dissenters and in particular against MCulloch.

Uniacke remained out of the debate until the question of public funding for the school arose. When it received £200 in 1814 he raised no objections in council, but the next year he combined with Croke to oppose another grant. Initially he had been enthusiastic for the school, but the hostility to the Church of England generated by the controversy greatly alarmed him. The school was under the patronage of Sherbrooke and later Dalhousie. For Uniacke to become an opponent of an institution under the governor's patronage would not have been easy and probably explains why his opposition was delayed. Nor was his opposition total as he remained on the governing committee for the school until his death.

Croke had been prepared to engage in public polemics with his adversaries, but Uniacke detested these as destructive of public harmony. His lack of scholarly training also precluded him from matching the erudition of Croke and McCulloch. Neither Uniacke nor Croke ever suggested that Anglicanism was in doctrine superior to other religions; the issue was political, not religious.[25] They did not question the right of Dissenters to practise their religion, but they believed that equality in law with the Church of England threatened the very basis of the British constitution.

In 1815, when the assembly resolution for a grant to the school came before council, it was initially refused, and then, while Croke and Uniacke were temporarily absent, it was resubmitted and hurriedly passed.[26] This was the first of a number of occasions when majorities in the assembly and council acting conjointly were able to out-manoeuvre unwelcomed opposition. Croke and Uniacke then jointly protested against the grant on the grounds that the established religion should be

---

25. Croke made this quite clear in his letter to McCulloch printed in the *Acadian Recorder*, October 2 and 9, 1813. This letter is the ablest defence for the principle of an established church made in Nova Scotia. McCulloch, who replied in the *Acadian Recorder* of November 6, 1813, was not really opposed to the principle, but was vehemently opposed to the claims of the established church to control education in a province in which the majority of inhabitants were not of the established church.

26. Protest by Croke and Uniacke, April 3, 1815, RG 1, Vol. 288, No. 108, P.A.N.S.

the foundation of any system of public education receiving legislative support. If pupils of the school were not required to attend church, this, they warned, could only lead to neglect of the Sabbath and dissipated conduct, and be destructive of all religion. They charged that the school was founded on latitudinarian principles which could only create "want of respect for the established forms of worship, and of the British government and constitution, which are closely connected with it."[27] Croke was no doubt the mind behind the charge of latitudinarism, which in England had become associated with Unitarians. One reason John Inglis had given for breaking away from the Bible Society had been that Unitarians were involved. Ironically, from what we know of Uniacke's religious beliefs, they seem to have been low church and devoid of any theological speculation, but of course emphatically trinitarian.

The upshot of the dispute was that the Royal Acadian School became primarily a fee-paying school for Dissenters, and Inglis accordingly founded the National School under complete Anglican control in 1816 for poor children. The quarrel over the Royal Acadian School not only began a religious war in Nova Scotia, but it also divided Anglicans, a division that culminated in the rupture of the St. Paul's parish in the next decade.

It was one thing for King's to exclude Dissenters, another for it to continue to receive grants from the assembly while its supporters resisted attempts by Dissenters to gain public funds for their colleges. An attack on this unjust and galling arrangement first came from the Presbyterians, led by McCulloch, who was the most inspiring teacher of any generation in Nova Scotia.[28] The dispute over Pictou Academy that now ensued between high church Anglicans and Secessionist Presbyterians was the most divisive issue until the struggle for responsible government began in the 1830's.

McCulloch had started a school in Pictou. From the beginning he saw in his school an embryo for a college that would be modelled on the liberal principles of Scottish universities and above all train native clergy for the Secessionist church. In 1815, with the cordial support of Governor Sir John Sherbrooke, Edward Mortimer, the wealthy and much respected member from Pictou, presented a memorial for the incorporation of trustees for an academy at Pictou to provide liberal education for persons of every religious denomination. At the next

---

27. Ibid.
28. For the most recent study of McCulloch, see S.E. McMullin, "Thomas McCulloch: The Evolution of a Liberal Mind" (unpublished PhD thesis, Dalhousie University, 1977).

session a bill was presented to incorporate Pictou Academy. It was clear that the bill would have little difficulty in the assembly, but would meet opposition in the council. Croke had retired but Uniacke's opposition could be expected. His son-in-law Thomas Jeffery was also an extreme churchman and would support any position Uniacke took. Then there was Michael Wallace, the provincial treasurer and stalwart supporter of the Church of Scotland. Wallace had never forgiven Pictou for his defeat by Edward Mortimer in the 1799 election and blamed the Secessionists for it. Other members were sympathetic, but were determined that the academy would not become a rallying point for Dissenters.

Mortimer, McCulloch and S.G.W. Archibald, a Secessionist who was beginning his rise to public prominence, approached Judge Brenton Halliburton to find a way to ease the bill through the council. Halliburton was married to John Inglis' sister, but his grandfather had been a minister in the Scottish church and this may well have accounted for his support of the academy. He would not give his support unless the academy would be expressly for Presbyterians. Its supporters, particularly McCulloch, intended it to be a Presbyterian institution, but feared resentment in the assembly if the act restricted it to Presbyterians. Agreement was reached whereby the bill introduced into the assembly would contain no religious tests, but would be then amended in council by Halliburton to require the trustees to belong to the Church of England or to subscribe to a declaration professing the Presbyterian Westminster Confession of Faith.[29]

It had been Mortimer who had suggested inclusion of the Church of England test to make the bill "more unobjectionable", although there was no expectation that Anglicans would ever become trustees. McCulloch had drafted the declaration for Presbyterians, while assuring Halliburton that the academy would only be for them. The amended bill passed council with a suspending clause and was approved by the British government the following year. Although there was no religious requirement for students, it was obvious to all that the academy was for Presbyterians. Methodists were only lukewarm to it because they were not Calvinists, and Baptists also because it was too far from the Annapolis Valley.

---

29. Brenton Halliburton to Robert Hay, July 2, 1831, CO 217, Vol. 153, P.R.O. Halliburton was in London attempting to explain for the benefit of the Colonial Office the complexities of the Pictou Academy dispute. For McCulloch's version see copy of his petition to the British government, c. 1828, MG 1, Vol. 554, No. 55, P.A.N.S. McCulloch claimed that Halliburton would not assist unless the academy was for Presbyterians only and that Archibald told him, McCulloch, to accept the changes and get them altered later.

Uniacke and Wallace had offered no opposition because it would be supported by private subscription, and they believed that by requiring tests for the trustees the "management and direction" would be confined to members of the Churches of England and Scotland as by law established.[30] They seemed to have been under the impression that by requiring Presbyterians to subscribe to the Westminster Confession of Faith only members of Church of Scotland could be trustees. Both knew that the Church of Scotland was not by law established in Nova Scotia, but the act was one way of gradually securing its establishment, and thus cementing Anglicans and Kirkmen (Church of Scotland adherents) in a church and state alliance to oppose the challenge of Dissenters more successfully. They were fully aware that the academy was for Presbyterian "seceders", but feared it would be "productive of mischief" if controlled by McCulloch and his fellow Secessionists.[31]

The Pictou Academy began operations; however, the need of funds soon drove it back into the political arena. In 1818 the trustees applied for a grant which Dalhousie supported in spite of the original understanding that no public funds would be requested. The assembly, however, agreed to a grant of £500 but attached a rider requiring £1000 in private subscription before payment. In council the request was refused outright.

Among Presbyterians there was dissatisfaction with the requirement that trustees declare their adherence to the Westminster Confession of Faith. In the 1819 session of the assembly, Archibald introduced a bill to repeal this test and substitute a simple profession to the Christian Religion according to Presbyterian principles and forms of the Church of Scotland. Dalhousie thought the change of little importance and a majority in the council agreed. Not Uniacke, who protested vehemently at what he saw as a betrayal of the "understanding that none of the various Sectaries... or any of the Seceders from the established churches of England and Scotland were to have any concern in the direction or management" of the academy. With Jeffery and Wallace, he charged that the change would make the academy a "point of union for all denominations of Dissenters, Seceders and Schismatics to unite in their operations to place themselves on an equal footing with the Church of England established in the Province".[32]

---

30. Protest of Uniacke, Wallace and Jeffery, March 31, 1819, RG 1, Vol. 289, No. 94, P.A.N.S.

31. Halliburton to Hay, July 2, 1831, CO 217, Vol. 153, P.R.O.

32. Protest of Uniacke, Wallace and Jeffery, March 31, 1819. There is no question that Uniacke wrote all the protests made over the Pictou Academy and marriage licences and Wallace and Jeffery simply signed them. Interestingly, this March 31st protest, with the original signatures, was given to the supporters of the academy and has turned up in the Pictou Academy papers, RG 14, Vol. 51, No. 9, P.A.N.S.

Hardly had the amendment passed than the council was faced with a resolution requesting a grant of £500 for the academy. Knowing how opposed Uniacke would be, the majority passed the resolution when he was in another room.[33] Again, with the support of Jeffery and Wallace, Uniacke tabled another protest. He chastized his fellow councillors for setting a precedent for all other Dissenters to set up similar claims for public aid to assist them in founding "exclusive" establishments such as Pictou Academy. This was a telling criticism and in the late 1820's the council resisted further grants partly for this reason.

As attorney general Uniacke was responsible for drafting the charter of the academy, which he had not yet done, and therefore in his opinion granting funds to the trustees was illegal. It was McCulloch who had delayed the charter until he could get the religious test for Presbyterians changed.[34] He seems to have miscalculated the opposition among his own supporters to the original test, and none of the trustees in fact seemed to have taken it, although they still continued to act. The following year Uniacke did draft the charter and when he presented it to Dalhousie, he presumptiously certified it "to be a draft of such a charter as I think the law will warrant the Governor in Chief to Grant under my hand".[35]

The charter made clear that the academy was for those professing the Presbyterian religion and desirous of educating their children in its tenets. The governor had the authority to refuse to approve any trustee or teacher whom he considered was not of good moral standing or not well affected to government. All by-laws had to be approved by him. By the time the charter was drafted McCulloch, ebullient with success in obtaining funds and the change in the religious requirement for trustees, was speaking openly about his "College".[36] One reason Dalhousie had supported the academy was that he had been "solemnly assured" by the academy's supporters that they wanted "a school and nothing but a school". When he had discovered McCulloch intended a college, he felt betrayed and charged that he did not know of "any man so little to be fathomed or trusted".[37] Uniacke, probably with no need

---

33. Protest by Uniacke, Wallace and Jeffery, April 2, 1819, RG 1, Vol. 289, No. 67, P.A.N.S.
34. McCulloch to the Rev. Dr. Mitchell, May 29, 1819, MG 1, Vol. 553, No. 8. In his letters to Mitchell, McCulloch did not disguise his intentions. For example December 9, 1815, ibid., No. 2, he remarked that "We have already made an attempt to establish an Academy in Pictou with a view of the interests of the church".
35. The charter and note to Dalhousie are in RG 1, Vol. 173, pp. 478-91, P.A.N.S.
36. McCulloch to Dr. Mitchell, June 14, 1819, MG 1, Vol. 553, No. 10, P.A.N.S.
37. Note from Dalhousie in August 1826 printed in the *Pictou Observer*, September 11, 1838.

of urging from Dalhousie, wrote in the charter that the education at the academy would follow that of the academies of Scotland. Ever the legal mind, Uniacke had drafted the charter to ensure virtual government control, restricted its educational role, and ensured its sectarian character. In the 1820's its opponents used the charter to fight McCulloch's attempts to turn it into a college and broaden its support among other Dissenters.

The main reason why Dalhousie had given a "flat refusal" to Pictou Academy becoming a college was that he was in the process of establishing his own non-sectarian college in Halifax. In 1817 the council unanimously approved the use of funds collected as custom duties at Castine, Maine during the British occupation in the War of 1812 for the establishment of Dalhousie College. The assembly voted additional funds, and the college was incorporated with all governors being either Anglican or Church of Scotland. Three of them were already on the board of King's, including the bishop. The new college was modelled after Edinburgh University, which being in Scotland, was not subject to any religious restrictions. The Church of Scotland saw the new college as an opportunity to establish a chair of theology, and such a chair was incorporated into the Dalhousie College bill in 1821.

Uniacke was an enthusiastic backer of Dalhousie College. Control was in the hands of the two established churches, and Dalhousie was to provide a more practical education than was available at King's with its stress on classical and literary training. This emphasis appealed to Uniacke, lacking as he did a classical education himself. It was his own practical bent that caused him to recommend the establishment of a professorship of agriculture for the new college with the holder residing at the Governor's Farm, to be turned into an experimental farm.[38] Nothing came of this; Dalhousie College rapidly ran out of funds and by 1823 consisted of an unfinished building on the Grand Parade in Halifax with no students. King's also was in severe financial difficulties. The governors in 1818 had unanimously recommended to the Archbishop of Canterbury that the exclusivist statutes be repealed, but he had refused. Even among Anglicans there was growing dissatisfaction with their sons having to subscribe to the Thirty-nine Articles. The obvious solution was a union of King's and Dalhousie and such an attempt was now to be made with Uniacke's full encouragement.

Committees from the respective boards were appointed in 1823 to draft a plan of union for a United College of King's and Dalhousie to be

---

38. Draft of An Act for founding a professorship of Agriculture and establishing by useful instruction and successful experiments a good system of rural economy. RG 8, Vol. 2, P.A.N.S.

located in Halifax. Their report was sent to Uniacke, who enthusiasti-
cally backed it as "a measure of great public utility", but warned Governor Sir James Kempt that the plan would encounter much opposition,
requiring a "great deal of persistent as well as skillfull management to
bring this object to favourable termination."[39] It was essential that he, as
attorney general, together with S.B. Robie, the solicitor general, be
directed to draft a bill as soon as possible. In January 1824 the King's
governors approved the plan and discussed bills prepared by both
Uniacke and Inglis. They were at variance, and Robie was directed to
find a compromise. They had already been sent to Dalhousie at
Quebec, and he had favoured Inglis' preamble but Uniacke's bill. In
drafting the final bill, Robie followed Dalhousie's suggestions. This was
then submitted to the Archbishop of Canterbury and the Colonial
Office.[40] The final plan called for a college government similar to
King's, with the president to be a churchman, but the professorships
open to any religion and no religious restrictions for students. An
Anglican divinity school would be part of the college, and the
arrangements for granting of degrees suggest that a Church of Scotland
chair of theology was planned.

As Uniacke had prophesied, opposition immediately arose from
Anglicans and Presbyterians. Within the King's board Blowers was
adamantly opposed to any union from the very beginning, and graduates
rallied to resist a union with the "Scotch Bastard of a University".[41] Even
Croke, from his retirement in England, wrote in opposition. McCulloch,
sensing rightly that union would preclude any further attempts to turn
his academy into a college and fearing Anglican control of the united
college, brought pressure upon Dalhousie, suggesting that the solution
for Dalhousie College was to place it "under the guardianship of the
presbyterians".[42] The Archbishop of Canterbury refused his consent
and with his refusal the union plan failed, but only just; in 1827 the
British government would grant a royal charter to King's College in
Upper Canada very similar to the Nova Scotian union bill. If Blowers and

39. Uniacke to J.W. Nutting for Kempt, November 26, 1823, MG 1, Vol. 926, No. 90,
    P.A.N.S.

40. RG 1, Vol. 433, Nos. 41½ and 41¾, P.A.N.S., Minutes, B.G.K.C., January 3 and 7,
    1824 and April 7, 1824; and Kempt to Dalhousie, February 11, 1824 and Dalhousie to
    Kempt, May 13, 1824, Dalhousie Papers, A 527, P.A.C.

41. William Blowers Bliss to Henry Bliss, May 18, 1824, MG 1, Vol. 1598, P.A.N.S. In
    earlier letter January 5, 1823, William Bliss noted that none of the governors of
    King's who voted for union had a classical education. For the opposition to union see
    letters by Blowers, Croke and Rev. William Cochran, miscellaneous, CO 217, Vol.
    143, P.R.O.

42. McCulloch to Dalhousie, c. 1823, MG 1, Vol. 553, No. 151, P.A.N.S.

others had not opposed the union so vehemently there is good reason to believe that the British government and the archbishop would have acceded and granted financial support. Again, it was divisions within the Anglican party that had blocked attempts to create one university for Nova Scotia.

Throughout the 1820's opposition in the council to Pictou Academy increased, as did the bitterness between high church Anglicans holding sway in the council and the Secessionists backed by a strong majority in the assembly. To add to the growing animosity a religious quarrel broke between Secessionists and Kirkmen in Pictou, which was exploited, if not instigated, by opponents of the academy in Halifax. Efforts by supporters to obtain a permanent grant similar to the one for King's and to allow it to award degrees were consistently refused by the council, although annual grants were made. The minority in council led by Uniacke in the previous decade had now become the majority. Only in 1828 was he again in the minority when the council amended an assembly bill to provide a permanent grant.[43] The majority were prepared to agree if all the trustees were government appointed and no teacher to be a trustee, thus eliminating McCulloch. But no religious restrictions would be required of the trustees and this was presumably the reason for Uniacke's opposition. The assembly refused to accept the amendments and the dispute continued to be the most divisive issue of the 1820's, developing into a concerted attack on the constitutional role of the council. The academy question was not put to rest until 1836, when McCulloch became the first principal of Dalhousie. By then Nova Scotians were absorbed in the struggle for responsible government, with the reformers gaining much of their strength from Dissenters embittered by the church and state battles of the previous decade.

The battle over Pictou Academy was paralleled by another over the restriction for the issuing of marriage licences to Anglican ministers. In Nova Scotia no marriage could be performed by a minister of any denomination without the publication of banns unless a licence had been granted by the governor, who in practice simply handed out blank forms to Anglican ministers who in turn passed them on to Dissenting ministers upon request and for a fee. Marriage by licence was purely an Anglican rule and the licence required that the marriage be performed according to the rites of the Church of England. Dissenting ministers, however, found their use convenient, particularly in Halifax.

No one more than Uniacke resisted with greater tenacity the attempts of Dissenters to gain the right to be married by licence according

---

43. J.L.C., March 22, 1828.

to their own rites. McCulloch had not been able to gain the full support of other Dissenters for his academy and in 1817, quite by accident while in Halifax, hit upon the issue of marriage licences. Once John Inglis had become rector of St. Paul's he had stopped the previous policy of simply handing over blank marriage licence forms to Dissenting ministers upon request. A colleague of McCulloch's in Halifax had applied for a licence for his servant and been refused by Inglis. McCulloch immediately seized on this and orchestrated opposition among Dissenting ministers throughout the province. In private correspondence he freely admitted he had "started the business for the purpose of attaching the methodist and baptist" clergy to his academy, and boasted how he had done the established church "a serious unjury".[44] He apparently never married by licence and saw the issue solely as a means of gaining support for his academy and as "a trial of strength" with the Church of England.

In 1818 most of the Dissenting ministers petitioned the assembly to be allowed to marry by licences issued to them directly by the governor and to perform the ceremony according to their own rites. To have to obtain licences through an Anglican minister was "repugnant" and an infringement of their rights.[45] There was much confusion over the laws governing licences and the assembly decided not to pass an act, but to request Dalhousie to grant licences to Dissenting ministers authorizing them to celebrate marriages according to their own rites. Dalhousie had no recourse but to turn to Uniacke as principal law officer for an opinion.

Uniacke told him that as governor he had ecclesiatical duties entrusted to him by his royal instructions and he had to conform to the rules and regulations of the established church. Marriage by licence was solely a Church of England rule and the governor had no power to interfere with Protestant churches in celebrating marriages according to their own rules.[46] Uniacke, none too subtly, was making the point that the rules of Dissenting churches did not provide for marriage by licence, only by banns. He well knew this rule was often disregarded, but this was of no importance to him when he believed the established church was in danger.

When the assembly met in 1819 Dalhousie sent a message stating that he was bound by oath to preserve the forms and stipulations that the Church of England directed him to pursue. Undaunted, the

---

44. McCulloch to Dr. Mitchell, May 29, 1819 and November 10, 1822, MG 1, Vol. 553, Nos. 8 and 18, P.A.N.S. In his May 29 letter he described Uniacke as one of our "violent enemies".

45. Petition submitted February 25, 1818, RG 5, Series P, Vol. 1, 1818, P.A.N.S.

46. Uniacke to Dalhousie, June 3, 1818, Vertical Manuscript File: Uniacke, Richard John, Marriage Licences, 1818, P.A.N.S.

assembly, led by Archibald, passed a bill granting Dissenting ministers the right to marry by licence according to their own rites. During the debate it was made clear that the governor had acted on the opinion of Uniacke, an opinion challenged by Archibald but supported by W.H.O. Haliburton, the father of the author Thomas Chandler Haliburton.[47] However there was a clear majority favourable to the bill and with some amendments it passed in council with Uniacke, Wallace and Jeffery dissenting. The majority in the council was in league with the majority in the assembly and both groups knew that opposition would come from Uniacke. They rushed the bill through council, overriding Uniacke's objections. Uniacke, with the support of Wallace and Jeffery, then tabled the first of the least seven dissenting opinions, three of which the council refused to enter into its journals.[48]

Uniacke saw in the bill not only a desire by Dissenters for equality, but as an attack on the very principle of an established church. He believed that no good government could long exist without an established religion, and in one of his rhetorical flourishes told his fellow councillors that if the bill should become law, "the final overthrow of the church must follow and with it the constitution of our forefathers must perish".[49]

The plan of the supporters of the bill was first to override Uniacke's opposition and then to get Dalhousie to sign the bill into law without a suspending clause. Uniacke in his usual didactic style lectured the council on its duty to act in accordance with the king's instructions and not to submit to the popular will. Dalhousie, who had his own reservations about the bill, refused to sign without a suspending clause. A new bill containing a suspending clause was quickly passed with the aim of neutralizing Uniacke's opposition. To support the bill, which now had to receive the sanction of the British government, the supporters of the bill drafted an address giving the reasons why it should become law. Uniacke was now almost completely isolated; Wallace and Jeffery, although voting with him in council, no longer signed his dissenting opinions. Nevertheless, he was neither "terrified nor alarmed at the general union of dissenters" with which he was threatened and denied the existence of the "overwhelming numbers"

---

47. Assembly debates, *The Free Press*, March 9, 1819.

48. Uniacke to Dalhousie, April 14, 1819, RG 1, Vol. 289, No. 90, P.A.N.S. Uniacke enclosed three protests that he wished transmitted to the British government but Dalhousie refused to take any official notice of them because they were not entered on the council's journals.

49. Protest by Uniacke, Wallace and Jeffery, April 14, 1819, RG 1, Vol. 289, No. 93, P.A.N.S. The protest is corrected in Uniacke's hand.

of which he had heard so much, while claiming that Anglicans exceeded in numbers any other denomination.[50] At the Colonial Office the high church Tory Bathurst disallowed the act.

The united majorities in the council and the assembly, both containing many Anglicans, did reflect the popular will, but the right of Dissenters to marry by licence without any restrictions was not gained until 1834. Although Dalhousie had his reservations, it was Uniacke's opposition that ensured the bill would go to London without unanimous support. This could well have swayed the British government to accept sooner than it did that the continuation of the privileges of the imperial church were not necessary to ensure loyalty and were unacceptable to the majority of Nova Scotians. An annoymous writer to the *Acadian Recorder* summed up Uniacke's role when he said that it was likely that "hostile influence will be employed" to ensure disallowance in England of the marriage act.[51]

Nothing was to drive Uniacke to greater fury than the attempt by the Anglican congregation of St. Paul's to secure the right to choose its own rector. When its rector John Inglis was promoted bishop in 1824, the dispute over whether the Crown or the parishioners had the right of nominating the rector of St. Paul's rent the parish apart. It resulted in the founding of the Granville Street Baptist Church, and former parishioners, such as J.W. Johnston, J.W. Nutting and E.A. Crawley, provided the Baptists with a respectability and a leadership that would turn them into a major political and religious force. The dispute aroused Uniacke's Erastianism to a fever pitch, as he came to believe that the fate of the church establishment in British North America hung in the balance. His ruthlessness and the use of his position as attorney general engendered so much bitterness that St. Paul's was left a "mere wreck of its former self".[52] Many were driven into the Baptist church who would have given the church its lay leadership in the next generation.

In the Church of England the Crown, or others who granted land or funds to erect or endow a church, had the right to nominate or "present" the minister. Once presented, the bishop then inducted him

---

50. Protest by Uniacke, n.d., RG 1, Vol. 289, No. 91, P.A.N.S. The protest was initially written in the third person plural but changed later to the first person singular and only signed by Uniacke.

51. Observer in *Acadian Recorder*, February 7, 1824. The letter refers to the passage in the 1824 assembly session of a similar marriage bill. The council gave it the three month hoist.

52. Reginald V. Harris, *The Church of Saint Paul in Halifax, Nova Scotia* 1749-1949 (Ryerson, Toronto, 1949) p. 71.

into his spiritual charge as well as into the temporalities of the church. In Nova Scotia, until the arrival of Bishop Charles Inglis in 1787, the governor performed all these functions. Even after the appointment of Inglis, the governor retained the right to present.

Under its first rector, John Breynton, St. Paul's was low church and its congregation assumed that the right of presentation rested with it. When Breynton retired he secured an opinion from the law officers in London substantiating the parish position. His successor, Robert Stanser, was nominated by the Crown, but the secretary of state of the time hoped that the parish would accept Stanser, which it did.[53] There were no further difficulties until Bishop Charles Inglis died in 1816. Inglis had intended his son to succeed him but the British government was prevailed upon by a joint address of the assembly and council to appoint Stanser as bishop. The parish of St. Paul's passed a resolution assuring the British government that it would acquiesce in any appointment to St. Paul's, and John Inglis was nominated rector as expected. Bathurst told Governor Sir John Sherbrooke that he wanted Inglis presented in a manner that upheld the right of presentation by the Crown. Sherbrooke did present Inglis but he warned Bathurst he had no doubt that the prevailing opinion was that the right of presentation was vested in the parish.[54]

Inglis' high church views were in illfavour with some of his congregation and they found a spiritual leader in the popular curate Thomas Twining. Twining, who may have been mildly Calvinistic, was a member of an evangelical group that rejected the formalism of the Church of England. The group included Uniacke's son, Robert Fitzgerald, who was converted and decided to train for the ministry. Another awakened soul was Hibbert Binney, who went around visiting the young ladies of Halifax enquiring "if they have felt no symptoms of conversion, no inspirations or sudden calls to reform".[55] Uniacke was much in favour of his son entering the church, but it is doubtful if he approved of the evangelical fervour of Binney, his son and others. Living at the Mount in semi-retirement, he probably only attended St. Paul's occasionally and believed that Inglis had everything under control. He didn't.

In 1824, while John Inglis and Governor Sir James Kempt were both in England, Stanser resigned. There was no question that the

53. Grenville to Parr, June 7, 1791, CO 218, Vol. 27, P.R.O.

54. Sherbrooke to Bathurst, June 20, 1816, private, CO 217, Vol. 98, P.R.O.

55. William Blowers Bliss to Henry Bliss, April 13, 1818, MG 1, Vol. 1598, P.A.N.S. Young William thought Binney's sermons a "fine time for napping".

promotion would go to Inglis, but Kempt and Inglis warned Bathurst that the appointment of Inglis' successor at St. Paul's should be made as soon as possible to avert a "canvass" in Halifax.[56] Robert Willis at Saint John, New Brunswick, was the senior clergyman in the diocese and Bathurst chose him. The appointment entailed new arrangements in the diocese and Uniacke's son, Robert Fitzgerald, obtained St. George's in Halifax.

Before Bathurst had notified Michael Wallace, the administrator in the absence of Kempt, Inglis had written to Halifax in September that a vacancy at St. Paul's would likely occur. Twining, who had been acting as rector in the absence of Inglis, was very popular, and his supporters were determined that he should become the next rector. A special meeting of the churchwardens, vestry and parishioners was called in October to organize a petition supporting Twining. James Stewart, a justice of the Supreme Court, told Twining to call on Uniacke to determine his opinion. Uniacke told Twining that "if Government should arbitrarily send out a Rector to this country without consulting the wishes of the people saying 'there's your Rector' he . . . would be one of the first persons to kick against it".[57] He was prepared to sign a testimonial as to his character, but when Twining brought him the document, Uniacke refused to sign, claiming that the wording suggested it was somewhat more than a testimonial.

The official notification of Willis' appointment arrived in early November, and on the fifteenth and seventeenth November there were parish meetings and resolutions passed, claiming the right of presentation and electing Twining as rector. The right of the Crown to present, even on a promotion to a bishopric, was disputed on the grounds that it could not exist in a distant colony.[58] This direct challenge to the imperial church and state relationship was further confirmed when the churchwardens refused to induct Willis, although ordered by Wallace, arguing that they had received no reply to petitions sent to Bathurst and Inglis. Wallace then arranged to have Willis inducted by the Rev. Benjamin Gray, who placed Willis' hand on the locked door of St. Paul's.

---

56. Kempt to Wilmot Horton, September 22, 1824, and Inglis to same, September 14, 1824, CO 217, Vol. 143, P.A.N.S.

57. The answer of the Rev. John Thomas Twinning in the Court of Chancery, The Attorney General versus the Rev. John Thomas Twinning, RG 36, Vol. 31, No. 680, P.A.N.S.

58. Petition of the Church Wardens, Vestry and Parishioners of the Parish of St. Paul's to the King in G.W. Hill "History of St. Paul's Church, No. III, *Collections*, N.S.H.S., Vol. III, pp. 23-5 (hereafter Hill, No. III).

Uniacke was enraged by these developments. As attorney general he now took control of affairs on behalf of the government, evincing a determination and a ruthlessness that belied his seventy-two years. He wanted no help, as he wrote Inglis, but that the government should stand firm in its measures with the "same obstinate pertinacity" as its opponents, because the King had proceeded too far to admit of any compromise short of submission. The fate of the church establishment in British North America hung "on the event, and the least shadow of success which a tempouring [sic] system on our part would manifest, would be a signal for the same principles to operate in every part".[59] To assist in undertaking legal proceedings, he called in his son Richard John and S.G.W. Archibald; the latter initially had become involved in the proceedings on behalf of the parish, but Uniacke reminded him that this might be "ruinous to himself and his family".[60] He considered Twining, unfairly, to be responsible for disrupting the harmony of the parish and threatened that he would take legal steps to have him either silenced or suspended for pretending as a minister of the Church of England. In a letter to Inglis he accused Twining of acquiring influence "by an external appearance of affected holiness clothed with all the terrors which the gloomy tenets of Calvin are calculated to produce".[61] Twining was not yet overborne by the forces brought against him and told Uniacke that his resentment and bad language towards him were "inconsistent with the character of a Christian".[62]

Uniacke's full fury was directed against the "Democratic Demogogues ... a species of noxious animal with which I shall be at war as long as I live", as he called the churchwardens who opposed Willis' induction.[63] He accused them and their supporters of attempting to introduce "Mob Government" into the civil and religious systems and of trying to "throw the whole Administration ...of the Church ... into the hands of the people". The parish meetings called were considered by him illegal and "promiscuous" assemblies and an attempt to make the authorities yield to the "howlings of an agitated Mob".[64] The accusation that his son's appointment to a parish was a

---

59. Uniacke to Inglis, January 3, 1825, a letter copied by Mr. C.E. Thomas from a group of letters entitled the "Uniacke Letters" in the records of St. Paul's, which appear to be no longer extant (hereafter the Uniacke Letters, St. Paul's), P.A.N.S.
60. Uniacke to the Church Wardens, April 21, 1825, letter copied by Mr. C.E. Thomas from the records of St. Paul's, Twinning — Willis Controversy, P.A.N.S.
61. Uniacke to Inglis, February 12, 1825, Uniacke Letters, St. Paul's, P.A.N.S.
62. Twinning to Uniacke, January 4, 1824, Uniacke Letters, St. Paul's, P.A.N.S.
63. Uniacke to the Church Wardens, January 6, 1825, Twinning — Willis Controversy, St. Paul's, P.A.N.S.
64. Uniacke to Inglis, February 12, 1825, Uniacke Letters, St. Paul's, P.A.N.S.

reason for his opposition to the wishes of the congregation stung him to reply that he would rather see his son "doomed to beg his daily bread in our streets for the residue of his life than see him enjoying the highest stations in the church, if obtained in opposition to the will of the King who on earth is the Supreme Head of the Church of England".[65]

In February 1825 Uniacke filed suit in Chancery against Twining and the churchwardens and vestry of St. Paul's. Twining did not file an answer until March and the churchwardens and vestry never did so. Meanwhile, in England the law officers of the Crown considered the right of presentation was in ordinary cases vested in the parishioners, but upon a vacancy occasioned by the promotion of the incumbent to a bishopric the right of presentation was the Crown's.[66] This opinion was transmitted to the parish with a warning that if there was any further opposition, legal proceedings would have to be undertaken. These Uniacke had already begun.

The parish capitulated in April, but not before passing resolutions supporting the right to nominate its rector and that their just claim had been "violently threatened" and the "contest rendered unequal only by superior influence opposed to them".[67] A majority voted to withdraw from the church and immediately to procure another place for divine worship. Uniacke attended this meeting and voted with the minority against all the resolutions, as well he might, considering that the "superior influence" was a reference to himself. Twining, who had been conducting services at the request of the church wardens and vestry, served notice that he would discontinue to do so. At another meeting, the majority decided that the churchwardens should not induct Willis, but he was to have the liberty of entering the church. The majority then withdrew from the church, but it divided, with a substantial number attempting to set up a proprietary chapel with Twining as their minister, and the remainder going to St. George's. A proprietary chapel was one independent of the bishop and diocese.

Shortly after the chapel was formed Twining refused to serve; the congregation joined the Baptists forming the Granville Street Baptist Church. Those who went to St. George's included Beamish Murdoch and T.C. Haliburton, both of whom were fierce critics of Inglis. Uniacke and his son Richard John joined them and the church was

65. Uniacke to the Church Wardens, January 6, 1825, Twinning — Willis Controversy, St. Paul's, P.A.N.S.

66. Law Officers to Bathurst, March 10, 1825, miscellaneous, CO 217, Vol. 145, P.R.O.

67. Meeting of the Church Wardens, Vestry and Parishioners, April 13, Hill, No. III, p. 62.

removed from the control of St. Paul's by the erection of a new parish in 1827. Over Uniacke's opposition, Inglis, through Kempt, arranged to have the proceedings in Chancery stopped, as they had been "productive of personal offence".[68] An anonymous letter writer to the *Acadian Recorder* summed up the popular feeling when he said that "Halifax is growing every day less aristocratical, and more disposed to judge of public measures by their utility, than by the interests of a few powerful individuals".[69]

Utterly convinced that the church establishment in British North America was threatened by the parishioners of St. Paul's who wanted the rector of their choice, Uniacke applied the full force of the law against them. He won a legal victory for the established church, but the violence and tenacity with which he pursued the cause inflicted a wound on the parish from which it would never fully recover.

When Uniacke considered a cause was just however, as he did Catholic emancipation, he could be remarkably flexible and politic. No one was more pleased than he when Edmund Burke in 1819 became the first Catholic bishop of Nova Scotia. At the Charitable Irish Dinner of the same year, he praised Burke "in a very animated" speech. (Burke, of course, had no love for McCulloch and the Secessionists and at the time of his death a year later was composing another polemic against them.) Demands for Catholic emancipation were intensifying in Nova Scotia and in England, and with these the Uniackes as a family were in full sympathy.

After the reuniting of Cape Breton to Nova Scotia in 1820, Richard John Uniacke and Lawrence Kavanagh were elected to the assembly. Kavanagh was a Catholic and the question of what oath he should take became a problem for both the Nova Scotian and British governments.[70] Catholic justices of the peace had been taking the oath of 1783, and it was hoped that this oath could be used. Kavanagh did not appear for the 1821 session, thus allowing time to consult with the British government. Bathurst refused to allow the 1783 oath to be taken, but left the door open for a change of policy. In 1822 the assembly passed a bill to abolish the declaration against transubstantiation, but the council on the urgings of Uniacke and Brenton Halliburton wanted to proceed somewhat more indirectly. Both were very conscious of the difficulties facing the British government because of the bitter debate over

---

68. Inglis to Kempt, January, 1826, MG 1, Vol. 481, P.A.N.S.

69. Letter from William Tell, *Acadian Recorder*, December 25, 1824.

70. For the question of the oath, see John Garner, "The Enfranchisement of the Roman Catholics in the Maritimes", *CHR*, Vol. 34, No. 3, pp. 203-18.

emancipation in England. A petition was sent to the British government on behalf of Kavanagh, and Bathurst agreed to make an exception. In the 1823 session Richard John moved that Kavanagh be admitted using the 1783 oath, and he took his seat. In 1827 Richard John presented a petition of one thousand Catholics, drafted in his father's office, requesting a dispensation from the declaration. This resulted in an address to the King by the assembly. The British parliament was still embroiled in the Catholic emancipation debate and it was not until 1829 that emancipation was finally granted. This was followed by a Nova Scotian Act the following year. Irish Catholics in Halifax would long venerate the memory of Uniacke for his efforts on their behalf. During his lifetime a toast was offered to him at the Charitable Irish Society Dinners for "His eminent service in the cause of equal civil and religious Freedom".[71]

Uniacke's Erastian convictions did not derive from his belief that the doctrine of the Church of England was the only true Christian one. Doctrine was of little importance to him and doctrinal disputes only weakened Christianity in its struggle with atheism, infidelity, superstition and idolatry, the evils he saw shaking civil and religious society to its very foundations. He despised the corruption of the 18th century Anglican church and probably looked with some envy upon the religious commitment and energy of Dissenting and Catholic clergy in Nova Scotia. His opposition to Dissenters did somewhat mellow because, as he told Kempt in 1822, he had come to the opinion that "the established religion receives a serious injury whenever any impediment on the part of the government is shown in the way of any other religious sect". This opposition he found had only produced "an increase of zeal and enthusiasm accompanied with feelings of vindicative treatment of the established church".[72] What he feared in the Dissenting churches was not their doctrine but the democratic character of their government. When St. Paul's wanted to nominate its own rector, Uniacke saw his own church succumbing to mob government. The issue for him was never a local one, but involved a threat to the very existence of the church establishment in British America. It was a challenge to the very being of the established church over which the King was the supreme head.

As with his constitutional views, it was not what was actually happening in Nova Scotia that caused him to oppose with such

---

71. Records of the Charitable Irish Society, MG 20, Vol. 65, P.A.N.S.

72. Uniacke to William Hill (deputy provincial secretary) August 25, 1822, MG 1, Vol. 926, No. 90, P.A.N.S.

vehemence the desire of Dissenters to secure equality with the Church of England, but rather that he associated their desires with the contagion of revolutionary principles that he saw spreading throughout the civilized world. He could never accept that Dissenters such as McCulloch believed as much as he did in a Christian society. He interpreted their desire for equality as no less than a revolutionary challenge and reacted accordingly. In the process he did much to retard necessary educational advances and divide Nova Scotian society along religious lines. And as he came to accept when much damage had been done, the established church received only injury from opposing the desire for religious and educational equality.

Chapter Six

Bed of Procrustes

Uniacke was sixty-seven in 1820 and lived as vigorous a life as ever to the end of the decade. His health remained robust, his intellect unimpaired and his love of life still strong and flowing. The remainder of his children reached adulthood at this time and he did his utmost to secure their happiness. He accepted the inevitable approach of death with an increase of his concern to ensure that there would be no friction within his family after his death. In his will, written in 1823, he left the Mount to his eldest son, with the provision for it to be passed to each succeeding son if the eldest did not wish it. The remainder of his estate was divided equally among his other eleven children, and for his second wife he purchased a home in Halifax. Andrew, his youngest, was still a student at King's College, and in a letter to his children to be opened after his death he urged his older children to take as warm an interest in Andrew's welfare as he had done for them.[1] In fact, he lived to see Andrew enter his law office as a student.

He lived most of the year at the Mount, coming to town only for council meetings and to attend to the duties of attorney general. S.B. Robie and later S.G.W. Archibald, as solicitors general, often substituted for him in prosecuting cases for the Crown; this drew some criticism from hopeful successors, who on occasion displayed unbecoming eagerness for his resignation or death. His great ambition was to become chief justice, and he assumed this place would come to him because of his seniority. There were, however, others who believed they should have the appointment, and the result was one of the most distasteful contests for office in the history of Nova Scotia.

This unseemly scrambling for office played a significant role in the dispute over revenue bills and the Brandy Election of 1830. Uniacke attempted to moderate between the council and the

---

1. Uniacke to My Dear Children, November 11, 1823, Vertical Manuscript File: Uniacke, Richard John, Will. 1823, P.A.N.S.

assembly, and there was none of the fanatical opposition he had displayed in the church and state debates. Having been involved in conflicts between the council and assembly over money bills since 1784, he understood only too well the passions that could be aroused and what would be the final result.

The Nova Scotian version of the controversy over money bills was symptomatic of the agitation against entrenched colonial oligarchies throughout British America. In all the colonies there were increasing demands that governments become more responsive to public opinion, but colonial constitutions had been designed to inhibit the growth of democracy by ensuring that permanent officials did not come under the control of elected assemblies and by making appointed councils an integral part of the legislative process. Councillors were chosen not for their representativeness but for their loyalty and conservatism. Although appointed at the King's pleasure, they generally retained their seats for life, while governors came and went. They came to consider themselves less as trusted advisers to the governor than as the natural governors, while at the same time attempting to impose a hierarchical structure on societies increasingly democratic in character.

By the 1820's no one in British America had had more experience in trying to make the colonial government work than Uniacke. He shared none of the complacency of his fellow councillors that democratic forces could be contained within the colonial constitutions which they found so furthered their interests. In a letter to Dalhousie in 1821, who was grappling with the quarrels between the French controlled assembly and the English faction entrenched in the council and public offices, he compared colonial constitutions to the "bed of procrustes" because they were so inapplicable to local conditions.[2] (The fabulous giant Procrustes of ancient Greece had fitted his captives to his bed by stretching and mutilating them.) Uniacke wrote to Dalhousie at Quebec that he felt hopeless about the future fate of the colonies and that the whole system of colonial government seemed "ruled by unalterable destiny which appears gradually leading to those great changes which providence always brings about through an apparent natural cause of ordinary events". He was not as fatalistic as his words suggest and out of his seminal mind would come the most prescient proposals for colonial constitutional reform until the Durham Report of 1839.

After his arrival in Quebec, Dalhousie had appointed the speaker

2. Uniacke to Dalhousie, July 20, 1821, Dalhousie Papers, A527, P.A.C.

of the assembly, Louis Joseph Papineau, to the executive council in an attempt to gain support for his government in the assembly. In this decision he may well have been influenced by a paper read in council by Uniacke in 1819. There had been separate executive and legislative councils in the Canadas since 1791, and Uniacke had recommended in his 1806 memoir to the Colonial Office that separate councils be created in Nova Scotia. In 1819 he once again argued that a legislative council should be established and made up of well-informed persons of property and influence from throughout the province. He told his fellow councillors that they were not devoting enough time to their legislative responsibilities, and because their proceedings were not open, there was an "almost universal opinion" that they were not fulfilling their duties.[3] Uniacke never saw himself as a member of an oligarchy, but as a faithful and trusted servant of the Crown. He had no illusions about his colleagues and never hesitated to remind them of what he considered their duties.

In his paper, however, he went further in articulating a solution to that critical deficiency of colonial constitutions, the lack of any bridge between the executive branch and the assembly. In England the cabinet system was taking form and the King's ministers sat either in the House of Commons or the House of Lords and could present, and defend, government policy. Although in the 1790's the occasional member of a colonial assembly had been also a member of the executive council, the assemblies had looked upon such appointments as an intrusion by the executive to be guarded against. Uniacke wanted the governor to call members of both the assembly and the legislative council who, with a number of high officials, would form the executive council. The governor would then have the best talents and general information available and "that reasonable weight and influence in both branches of the legislature, the want of which must be nonsensibly [sic] felt". In no sense did Uniacke believe that executive councillors should be responsible to the popular branch; on the contrary, their loyalty was to the governor and their duty to advise him and carry on his government. His fellow councillors simply ignored his proposal; however, a variation of it appeared in the 1822 parliamentary bill to unite the Canadas.[4]

In the past Uniacke had argued for two strong governments in

---

3. Minutes of Council, Aprill 22, 1819, RG 1, Vol. 215, P.A.N.S.

4. The bill provided for two councillors to sit in the assembly but they could not vote. See K.L.P. Martin, "The Union Bill of 1822", *C.H.R.* Vol. 5, No. 1 (March 1924) p. 45.

British America, but in his letter to Dalhousie he first put forward his idea of a union of all the colonies. Such a union had first been suggested in 1785, and again in 1790, by the loyalist William Smith who later became chief justice of Lower Canada.[5] Smith, like many loyalists, had believed that if a union of all the American colonies had been formed the rebellion would have been avoided. In 1754 delegates of the American colonies had gathered in Albany, New York to draft a plan of union but had been unable to reach agreement.[6] Loyalists were familiar with the Albany Union Plan, however, and Uniacke probably gained his knowledge of it from the Nova Scotian loyalist Foster Hutchinson, whose uncle, Thomas Hutchinson, the last royal governor of Massachusetts, had attended the Albany meeting. Whether Uniacke knew of Smith's plans is not known, but he did have knowledge of the Albany Union Plan and drew on it for his own union scheme for British America.

Uniacke believed that if, at the end of the American War, a general government had been instituted over the whole of the remaining North American colonies, all the evils that had arisen in colonial government would have been avoided. In 1821 he does not seem to have envisaged a federal union, but rather a legislative one in which there would be only one general legislature composed of an elected lower house and an appointed upper house with local administration under the responsibility of lieutenant governors. Under a general union he was convinced British America could secure the commerce of the world and "constitute a vast and powerful superior nation" with advantages such as no other portion of the earth possessed.[7] This theme of potential greatness of British America underlaid his belief in the necessity for union.

The union of Upper and Lower Canada was being discussed as a means of solving the dispute between them over the distribution of customs revenue and the racial divisions in Lower Canada. It was the English faction in Lower Canada that was more in favour of union, and saw it as the only way to offset the power of the French. Uniacke despised the English faction in Lower Canada and accused them of trying to establish a hereditary nobility and perpetuate their monopoly of power while arrogantly assuming the French peasantry

---

5. See L.F.S. Upton, *The Royal Whig: William Smith of New York and Quebec* (University of Toronto Press, Toronto, 1969) pp. 157-8 and 203-4 for Smith's proposals.

6. See L.H. Gipson, *The British Empire Before the American Revolution*, Vol. V (Alfred A. Knopf, New York, 1942) pp. 128-42.

7. Uniacke to Dalhousie, July 20, 1821.

would never "presume to conceive a will of their own".[8] However, the Canadians had discovered the power of numbers and gained control of the assembly, and now were prepared to vote funds to cover the salaries of government officials, thus gaining control over them. To Uniacke this was of course an insidious proposal, but he blamed the English faction and told Dalhousie that the continued exercise of "negative powers" over money bills by the Lower Canadian council would lead to the triumph of the assembly. The only solution was the establishment of a union and effficient government over all the colonies.

French Canadian Nationalism was contemporary with the move for Catholic emancipation in Ireland, and Irish nationalists were deeply interested in affairs in Quebec. Uniacke's Irishness, as well as his support of Catholics in Nova Scotia, probably accounted in part for his sympathetic attitude towards the aspirations of French Canadians. In this he was perhaps unique among "British" North Americans. His son Norman had become attorney general of Lower Canada in 1809 and the English faction had never ceased in their efforts to have him removed and have one of their own succeed him. A year after Norman was appointed he had been temporarily superseded and only the intervention of Lord Liverpool, then the secretary of state responsible for the colonies, had ensured his reinstatement. Uniacke had brought all his influence to bear to have Liverpool intervene. Norman's tenure as attorney general was fraught with difficulties and his empathy for French Canadians only increased the anger of the English "junta", as his father called the English faction. He returned home to Halifax on a two-year leave of absence in 1819, and Uniacke's attitude towards French Canadians was greatly influenced by the experiences and views of his son.

Before Dalhousie's departure to assume the governor generalship, he must have consulted Norman about Lower Canada, particularly as Norman was now his principal law officer. Dalhousie's initial attempts to meet French Canadian grievances may well have been inspired by Norman. Certainly as soon as Norman returned to Quebec, the English faction made another attempt to have him removed. Dalhousie refused to do so; he was satisfied with Norman's performance of his duties. But Uniacke had always wanted his son to have a position in Nova Scotia and he now tried to secure the chief justiceship of Nova Scotia for him. Dalhousie, however, refused to superannuate Blowers and have Norman appointed.[9] Norman was promoted, much against his will, to

---

8. Ibid
9. Dalhousie to Uniacke, November 30, 1822, Dalhousie Papers, Vol. 5, P.A.C.

the Lower Canadian bench in 1825.[10] Just before this, as a member of the assembly, he voted for Papineau as speaker. The wrath of the English faction was so vehement that Norman thought he was ruined and went to London, where he was joined by his father, and both argued Norman's case at the Colonial Office. Norman never lost his sympathy for French Canadians, it should be said, and during the aftermath of the 1837 Rebellion used his position on the bench to restrain the "bloodhounds of prosecution".[11]

The British government was receptive to a union of the Canadas and in the summer of 1822 a union bill was presented to parliament, although it was quickly withdrawn when the opposition insisted that the Canadas should be consulted.[12] In anticipation that a new union bill would be introduced in the next session, Uniacke wrote a seventy page letter to Frederick Robinson, the President of the Board of Trade, giving his views on the absolute necessity for a general union of the British North American colonies.[13] His letter was written in haste and lacks the organization of his plan for a union submitted in person four years later. It was also written before the Huskisson reforms granting commercial freedom to the colonies, and a good part of it was taken up with the necessity for freeing colonial trade from the restraints of the trade and navigation laws.

He began his letter with a lengthy review of the innumerable evils that had befallen the colonies by the illegality and injustice of the dismemberment of old Nova Scotia and the division of old Quebec into Lower and Upper Canada in 1791. The failure of Britain after the conquest of Canada in 1763 to create a federal union of all her North American colonies and to grant commercial freedom had made the American Rebellion inevitable. Uniacke believed that only by a general union and the granting of such commercial freedom could the remaining colonies be saved from conquest by the United States or be able to withstand the onslaught of revolutionary principles. He both feared and envied the new United States, and events there greatly influenced his ideas on union and the necessity for it.

Much of Uniacke's information about the United States and that of

---

10. Robert Christie, *A History of the Late Province of Lower Canada* (Quebec 1850) Vol. III, p. 63.

11. Obituary of Norman Uniacke, Acadian Recorder, March 13, 1847. Norman became a member of the Nova Scotian Legislative Council in 1838 and supported the "popular" cause as did both Crofton and James Boyle Uniacke.

12. See William Smith, "The Attempted Union of 1822", *C.H.R.*, Vol. 2, No. 1 (March 1921) pp. 38-45.

13. Uniacke to Frederick Robinson, November 16, 1822, Board of Trade, 6/253, P.R.O.

his fellow Nova Scotians came from the New England Federalists, who were watching with alarm as corruption, party rivalry, lawlessness, and mob violence seemed to be overwhelming the enfeebled union. During the War of 1812, public and private papers found on captured prize ships had been seized, and Uniacke as an official of the Vice Admiralty Court had read much of this correspondence. Most of the captures were from New England; their owners and crews had been bitterly opposed to the war and this was reflected in the seized correspondence. This source of information was matched, and its Federalist bias accentuated, by the close commercial and family connections that Nova Scotians maintained with New England through peace and war.[14] Uniacke himself claimed to have had many correspondents in the United States, although no evidence has survived. The conservatism of post-loyalist Nova Scotia was reinforced by its contacts with Federalist America, although by the 1820's there was a new generation and it looked with more favour on American democracy.

In his letter to Frederick Robinson, Uniacke drew a clear distinction between what he called Old America and New America. The former comprised the commercial states of the eastern seaboard, which were Federalist in politics and had been opposed to the War of 1812; the New America embraced the southern and western states into which swarms of European immigrants were entering, all carrying with them the violent principles of the French Revolution. They immediately became citizens, able to vote and open to every enticement of demagogues. He called them half-savage barbarians, the outcasts of all nations, who scarcely felt "the power of the Government . . . as all power is derived from them by the elections".[15] These people Uniacke believed were uniting with the despicable slave owners of the south to ensure the election of their party, and would overwhelm Old America. The War of 1812 had been a war by the western states against British dominion in America, and it had been the dread of the western peoples that had caused the New Englanders, or Old America, not to support the war. In the 1820's he was in no doubt that the western states still held to a grand design of northern aggrandizement.

However Uniacke was less afraid of outright conquest than the growth of democracy, and the constitutional proposals he put forward to Robinson reflected this concern. In company with conservatives of his

---

14. An example, although pertaining to New Brunswick, is the correspondence between Attorney General Jonathan Bliss and his brother-in-law Thomas Dwight of Massachusetts, a leading Federalist politician in MG 1, Vol. 1607, P.A.N.S.

15. Uniacke to Frederick Robinson, November 16, 1822, p. 9.

age, he associated democracy with factions and party politics, a development that could only be destructive of constitutional government. Behind his conservatism and often exaggerated rhetoric was a very prescient, political mind. He foresaw that the projected union of the Canadas would lead to the growth of English and French parties. The governor would be forced to govern with the support of party and lose all his influence and independence, becoming "a tool in the hands of intriguers".[16] It was a "fixed principle" with Uniacke that the governor must be above faction and party if the King's government was to be carried on. As the history of the 1840's demonstrated in all the colonies, governors had either to govern through party or not at all, and by the end of this decade the old constitutions were replaced by responsible government.

Although in his 1821 proposals for union Uniacke had not been very specific, a year later, having given them much more thought, he called on Frederick Robinson to present an act to parliament to establish the Royal Confederation of the British American Colonies in America, incorporating a Nova Scotia restored to its ancient boundaries, Lower Canada, Upper Canada, and all the remaining British territory in North America from Newfoundland to the Pacific Ocean and to the North Pole. The new state would be governed by a Grand Council, a term he derived from the Albany Union Plan, which would consist of a governor general, a privy council, composed of high officials, an appointed legislative council and an elected house of representatives. In contrast to his 1821 scheme there would be provincial legislatures, but with very restrictive powers. The Royal Confederation was envisaged as a highly centralized state with control very much in the hands of the government. The new constitution was designed to ensure that monarchial principles would prevail and be the bulwark against republicanism, which he associated with that "ferocious animal", universal suffrage. Only a monarchial constitution he believed could avert a violent separation of the colonies from the mother country.

In 1814 the chief justice of Lower Canada, Jonathan Sewell, had submitted a proposal for a federal union to the Duke of Kent, but it was probably never forwarded to the Colonial Office.[17] Uniacke's plan for a Royal Confederation was the first one submitted as a consequence of the 1822 union bill. Others followed, notably that of John Beverley Robinson, the attorney general of Upper Canada, who was in London seeking a new arrangement for the distribution of revenue between the Canadas.

---

16. Ibid., p. 35.
17. R.G. Trotter, *Canadian Federation: Its Origins and Achievement, A Study in Nation Building* (J.M. Dent & Sons, London, 1824) p. 7.

He was opposed to a union of the Canadas and was asked in early January 1823 to submit a plan for a general union of the colonies. The timing of the request may be coincidental but it would have been within days of the arrival of Uniacke's letter. On the day that he was requested to submit a plan for a general union Robinson noted in his diary that his own plan "would go further than the suggestions I have seen".[18] He, of course, was familiar with the idea of a general union, but it remains a distinct possibility that he was shown Uniacke's letter to Frederick Robinson.

The thrust of the two plans and later that of the Rev. John Strachan was similar and derived from their shared Tory conviction of the necessity for strengthening the executive to meet the challenge of democratic and republican forces. The conviction was central to their plans for a general union. Where Uniacke differed from them was his passionate belief in the potential greatness of a British North American state and the emphasis which he placed on the complementary relationship between union and commercial freedom. Robinson and Strachan saw a general union as an alternative to a union of the Canadas in which French Canadians, because of their larger population, would gain a paramount influence.[19] Commercial freedom was of critical importance to Nova Scotia, with its seaborne trading interests, but Upper Canada was primarily concerned with obtaining its share of the customs revenue from Lower Canada, which it did under the Canada Trade Act drafted by Robinson.

The British government was moving towards granting greater commercial freedom to the colonies, and in early 1822 the Tory government of Lord Liverpool introduced five bills to repeal and simplify many of the navigation laws. The fourth bill was a major blow to the British American colonies and particularly Nova Scotia. It provided for the relaxation of the navigation laws in the interests of the West Indies by allowing direct trading with the United States. To offset the admission of American ships to the West Indies, duties were imposed on foreign commodities imported into the West Indies, whether imported in British or foreign ships. This gave the exports of British America an advantage over American. However, the colonies had little surplus in natural products to ship to the West Indies. This was most true of Nova Scotia whose trade with the West Indies, as always, depended upon being an entrepôt for American commodities, which were then re-exported to the

18. Major-General C.W. Robinson, Life of Sir John Beverley Robinson (Morang & Co., Toronto, 1904) p. 152-3, and see William Ormsby, "The Problem of Canadian Union", *C.H.R.*, Vol. 39, No. 4 (December, 1958) pp. 277-95.

19. The plans for union by Robinson, Strachan and Jonathan Sewell were published in *General Union of the British Provinces in North America* (W. Clowes, London, 1825).

West Indies. The entrepôt role of the free ports of the maritimes was destroyed by the act.

Robinson had been one of the ministers responsible for the act allowing direct American trading with the West Indies and nearly a third of Uniacke's letter to him was taken up in criticism of the act. Reflecting the views of contemporary economists, Uniacke lashed out at the old commercial system founded on monopoly as highly injurious to the mother country and ruinous to the colonies. In fact Robinson saw the 1822 acts as a start in reforming the old commercial system and no doubt agreed with the criticism of monopoly. However he viewed matters from the imperial perspective, in which the West Indies and trade with the United States were of far greater importance than trade with British North America. Uniacke could never accept this and wanted commercial freedom granted to the North American colonies and the monopoly of West Indian trade continued. The problems of the West Indies were caused by "the unbounded extravagance and destructive [sic] lavish and ill arranged system of management" and only the United States would benefit from the opening of the West Indies to direct trading.[20] Uniacke had a vision of a united British North America as an imperial partner offsetting the growing power of the United States; the West Indies in this vision were to remain a planters' colony, a class he had despised since he had first set foot in the West Indies as a youth of twenty.

The West Indies act in 1823 was a major disaster for the Halifax merchants, and worse was to follow; they discovered that the act prohibited them from importing sugar, molasses and coffee from foreign countries and colonies in the Americas, which was cheaper than importing them from the West Indies. The collector of customs was uncertain how the 1822 act should be interpreted, and the Halifax Chamber of Commerce asked Uniacke to give a legal opinion. This he did, supporting the right of the merchants to make such imports, and the practice was allowed to continue. However, when Uniacke's opinion was sent to the commissioners of customs in London, they replied that he was wrong and that such imports were illegal. Having acted upon Uniacke's opinion, the vessels and cargoes of the merchants who had engaged in the trade were now liable to seizure. It was most embarrassing for him but he was not prepared to change his opinion. He wrote a second opinion of much greater length justifying his original one, and Governor Sir James Kempt sent both of them to London. His legal arguments were complex and even James Stephen, the legal adviser to the Colonial Office, had some difficulty in following them.

---

20. Uniacke to Frederick Robinson, November 16, 1822, p. 20.

At issue was whether the 1822 act, which enumerated those articles that could be imported (and sugar, molasses and coffee had not been listed), had repealed previous acts that had regulated this trade with foreign countries in the Americas. Uniacke argued that the 1822 act had not done so, and even if it had, the colonies still had the "general right" to engage in this trade. Parliament could only regulate this trade, not prohibit it, as the colonies had it by "natural rights and immemorial usage".[21] As James Stephen pointed out, the 1822 act, by omission of the articles, had prohibited their importation, notwithstanding Uniacke's natural rights argument.[22] Uniacke's legal judgement had been swayed by his anger over the 1822 act itself. It was intolerable to him that the West Indies should not only have gained the right of direct trading with the United States, but that the British American colonies should also have to buy the higher priced West Indian goods because they were prohibited from buying elsewhere. As he had earlier told Frederick Robinson, "all reciprocity of interest" was at an end between the West Indies and the British American colonies.

Happily, in Britain the attack on the old commercial system intensified and legislation introduced by William Huskisson in March 1825 repealed all the existing navigation laws; the colonies were now free to trade as their commercial interests dictated. In place of monopoly and prohibition was substituted a system of imperial preferences that gave advantages to British manufacturers in colonial markets and to colonial staples in the British market. For Nova Scotians the injustice of the 1822 act had been undone. When the news of Huskisson's measures reached Halifax, public buildings were illuminated and a civic demonstration staged. For Uniacke the granting of the grand principle of free trade, as he called it, had "dissipated one of the darkest clouds that [ever] overshadowed the Commercial System of Great Britain".[23]

These views, given to the British government while he was in London in 1826, did not mean that he and the Halifax merchants were completely satisfied. Indeed, commercial relations with the United States were not settled by the 1822 and 1825 acts, because their implementation depended upon the United States removing discriminating duties on British ships and cargoes in American ports. The

21. Attorney General's second opinion to the Chamber of Commerce, Halifax enclosed in Kempt to Bathurst, August 30, 1823, CO 219, Vol. 142, P.R.O.

22. James Stephen to Wilmot Horton, November 13, 1823, CO 217, Vol. 142, P.R.O.

23. Observations on the British Colonies in North America with a Proposal for the confederation of the whole under one Government by Richard John Uniacke (Hereafter Observations, 1826) April 10, 1826, CO 217, Vol. 146, p. 463.

United States had not done this and the state of commercial war continued unabated. Uniacke was asked for his opinion by the Colonial Office. He reiterated his view that it was only necessary to allow American imports into the colonies free of duty for the re-export in British ships to the West Indies, where they should enter free of duty; imports direct from the United States should have to pay duty. In exchange for the American imports into British America, the Americans would obtain British manufacturers which they would smuggle into their own country. By this means the high duties charged on British ships and goods in American ports would be circumvented. Huskisson had already threatened to invoke measures to encourage smuggling, unless the Americans removed their discriminating duties. Such retaliatory measures continued until 1830, when an agreement was finally concluded.

Uniacke had decided in 1825 to go home once again to attend to his private affairs. During a nine month stay in England, Scotland and Ireland he remained in continuous touch with Robert Wilmot Horton, the undersecretary at the Colonial Office, a liberal-minded Tory who had the energy and intelligence so lacking in his superior, Lord Bathurst. It was at Horton's request that Uniacke appeared before the parliamentary Select Committee on Emigration, and it was with him that Uniacke discussed his ideas for a general union of all the colonies. Both were a consequence of his being in London and were not connected with his reasons for making a mid-winter Atlantic crossing in his seventy-second year.

During a visit to Nova Scotia in 1823, Dalhousie had noted that Uniacke seemed very low in spirits. The old attorney general, as Dalhousie fondly called Uniacke, threw a three day "riot" at Mount Uniacke for Dalhousie and his party as well as for notables from Halifax.[24] Upwards of twenty guests were accommodated with some sleeping on the billiard table and in the bath house. In the evenings Uniacke produced his Irish piper and all his servants and workmen assembled to dance with the guests. Back in Halifax Dalhousie was given a dinner at which 150 attended and Uniacke presided and "dealt his bumpers and his toasts around with great animation in order to cause . . . 'an excitment of the spirit'."[25]

The "riot" Uniacke had staged for Dalhousie had been a means of

24. Dalhousie's Journals, July 16, 1823 by the courtesy of Marjory Whitelaw who is editing them for Oberon Press.
25. Ibid., July 24, 1823.

raising his own spirits and thanking Dalhousie for his recent intervention on Norman's behalf. The attempted ouster of Norman had upset him very much, and for reasons not clear he also became desperately anxious about Crofton, who was practising at the English bar. The husband of his daughter Alicia had died in 1824, leaving her with young children to bring up and an indebted estate. Uniacke wrote numerous letters to his son James Boyle, who was studying law in London, directing him to act on behalf of his sister. Transatlantic mail often took months and waiting to hear about Alicia added greatly to his worries. Another daughter Anne was married and living in Ireland and she was in some financial difficulty.

Like any father whose children have gone off to live their own lives, he missed them and worried perhaps too much. Time was hanging very heavily on his hands, although in the summer months he kept himself amused with his country pursuits. Much of the winter he spent in town but found that "going so much into company" no longer was so agreeable to him; "retired tranquility" he believed best suited his time of life.[26] With concern for his family uppermost in his mind Uniacke in the late fall of 1825 made a sudden decision to cross the Atlantic once again. His decision may well have been precipitated by the death of his widowed daughter Lady Mary, who left one child for whom Uniacke was now responsible. Lady Mary had been in receipt of a pension since Sir Andrew Mitchell's death and Uniacke was anxious to have it passed on to the daughter. As he wrote his son Richard John after his arrival in London, he was determined to "lay a good foundation" for his family with the British Government.[27] Richard John was one of the many young lawyers attempting to make a living in a very overcrowded profession. Some, like J.W. Johnston and C.R. Fairbanks, were making over £800 a year but most were lucky if they got £100 and were desperate for the financial security provided by office. The pressure was somewhat relieved by the creation of three new judgeships in 1824, but this measure met much opposition, particularly when the three lawyers in the assembly who had vigorously supported the measure received the appointments. Uniacke "put his shoulder to the Wheel" in support of the new judgeships because he believed they would lay a good foundation for the legal profession and give greater stability to government.[28]

Blowers and Uniacke held the two most prestigious legal posts, and

26. Uniacke to his son James Boyle, April 3, 1824, MG 1, Vol. 926, No. 96, P.A.N.S.

27. Uniacke to his son James Boyle with a note for Dick, April 8, 1826, MG 1, Vol. 926, No. 94.

28. Uniacke to his son James Boyle, April 3, 1824.

both were old men. Blowers, now in his eighties, seldom presided in court. He left his duties to Justice Brenton Halliburton, who was anxious to succeed Blowers, as was S.G.W. Archibald. Uniacke assumed that he would succeed; the others hoped that age or death would remove him from the competition. Blowers had no intention of retiring to make way for his old rival and so in the mid-1820's it seemed that only death could intervene to open up opportunities for the young and aspiring of the Nova Scotian bar.

In 1823 when Uniacke had a nasty encounter with his pet bull, William Blowers Bliss immediately wrote his brother in London, who had contacts within the Colonial Office, asking him to secure the attorney generalship if Uniacke died.[29] What had happened was that Uniacke had forgotten to take some sugar to appease the bull when he patted him. The bull attacked, knocking him to the ground but Uniacke hit the bull on the nose with his stick and the bull did not make a second attack. His physical strength and presence of mind had saved him but he had been knocked about pretty severely. Bliss, who had married the adopted daughter of Blowers, was assured by his brother that he would get the attorney generalship if it became vacant. This was nonsense; Bliss was very junior and there were others, S.G.W. Archibald, for one, who had more senior claims.

From 1824 onwards there was a steady stream of Nova Scotian visitors to the Colonial Office anxious to secure offices for themselves and their sons. In an age before a permanent civil service was established and when pensions were seldom granted, securing office by influence and then holding it to death was accepted as normal. The first to cross the Atlantic in search of office was Archibald, who was followed in a month by S.B. Robie and C.R. Fairbanks, all to "watch" over each other.[30] Uniacke had never forgotten the role Archibald had played in Richard John's trial for murder and told his sons in London to give him every show of attention and provided him with a letter of introduction to his family in Ireland.

There was much speculation in Halifax as to why Uniacke decided to go to England once again. The general belief was that he intended to resign the attorney generalship to make way for his son Richard John to succeed him, but only after he had received a promise of the chief justiceship when it became vacant. Earlier, Uniacke had been prepared

---

29. William Blowers Bliss to his brother Henry, August 18, 1823, MG 1, Vol. 1598, P.A.N.S. Bliss tells the story of the encounter with the bull as does L.G. Power, "Richard John Uniacke", p. 115-6.

30. William Blowers Bliss to his brother Henry, March 28, 1824, MG 1, Vol. 1598, P.A.N.S.

to resign the attorney generalship and sacrifice the chief justiceship if Norman was appointed to succeed Blowers. He later denied that he ever solicited the chief justiceship at any time. This is probably true, as he assumed it would come to him by right of seniority and his long service to the Crown. His main concern was to secure positions for his sons Richard John and James Boyle. The competition was fierce and he wrote Richard John that he did not know how "his friends will stand the various calls on them". He was himself, the recipient of many applications by "persons of the first consideration" to secure offices for their numerous dependants.[31] The British government was not prepared to make any promises and would only appoint when vacancies occurred; so Uniacke had to be satisfied with the hope that his efforts would not go unrewarded in the future. Robie and Archibald were more successful; the former became the Master of the Rolls for Nova Scotia and the latter chief justice of Prince Edward Island while securing permission to reside in Nova Scotia. Archibald also succeeded Robie as solicitor general and speaker of the assembly.

While Uniacke was in London the provincial agent, Nathaniel Atcheson, died and he and Richard John used all their influence to secure the post for Crofton Uniacke. In Halifax Samuel Cunard and others wanted the London merchant, John Bainbridge, but Richard John won Fairbanks and Archibald over to the idea of appointing Bainbridge and Crofton as joint agents.[32] A resolution to this effect was presented by Fairbanks but lost by four votes in the assembly, primarily because the country members were opposed in principle to an agent in London. Within the council there was support for a third contender, Andrew Belcher, a former councillor and Halifax merchant who had lost much in the recent financial crash. Uniacke's friends on the council supported Crofton and as a compromise it was proposed to the assembly that Belcher and Crofton be appointed joint agents. The assembly refused and no agent was appointed until 1830 when Bainbridge was made sole agent.

Concern for Crofton's prospects at the English bar was one of the reasons Uniacke had come to London and he was relieved to find that these at least equalled his "sanguine expectations".[33] He travelled to Scotland to visit Alicia and was presumably able to sort out her affairs to his satisfaction before going to Ireland. There he had another reunion

---

31. Uniacke to his son James Boyle, April 8, 1826.
32. William Blowers Bliss to his brother Henry, March 15, 1826, MG 1, Vol. 1598, P.A.N.S.
33. Uniacke to his son James Boyle, April 8, 1826.

with his family and had Sir William Betham, the Ulster King of Arms and Principal Herald of All Ireland, draw up the Uniacke family pedigree and confirm the family arms and crest.[34] He never ceased to remind his Nova Scotian offspring that they came from an ancient and honourable family and he was determined to maintain the connection between the transatlantic branches. (A close connection was continued for some years after his death and has never been completely broken to this day, although in our own century, and after one thousand years, the Uniacke name has now disappeared from Ireland.)

Almost immediately after Uniacke had landed in England he sought interviews with Bathurst and Horton at the Colonial Office. Although he also obtained an interview with the Prime Minister, Lord Liverpool, he dealt primarily with Wilmot Horton, who canvassed Uniacke's views on the granting of mining charters in Nova Scotia, the utility of encouraging emigration to the colonies and British trade with the United States.

Three months after his arrival Uniacke presented his "Observations on the British Colonies in North America with a Proposal for The Confederation of the whole under one Government". Just over half the length of his letter to Frederick Robinson, the Observations had the succinctness so missing in the letter. Nor was there the despair so previously evident; he now wrote with confidence, displaying little of the exaggerated language that had been all too prevalent in the past. This confidence came from the passage of Huskisson's trade reforms, which Uniacke believed showed that Britain no longer viewed the colonies with a "selfish feeling of Monopoly".[35] Nothing now remained but to form a general confederacy of the North America colonies and to adopt measures to make the "United Provinces of British North America" into a great state and an equal and inseparable partner in a great empire. Providence had "destined such a country for some great and mighty purpose" and the time had come for laying its foundation.[36] Union would be an opportunity for Britain to show the world that good government could be established without violent revolution, and would allow Britain and her North American colonies to be forever united in bonds of affection and mutual interest.

What Uniacke was proposing was not just union but virtually complete internal self-government with only trade and external affairs to

---

34. The original document is in MG 1, Vol. 926, P.A.N.S. Sir William made a number of errors, see R.G. Fitzgerald - Uniacke," Some Old County Cork Families - The Uniackes of Youghal", J.C.H.A.S., Vol. 3, No. 36, p. 254.

35. Observations, 1826, p. 463.

36. Ibid., p. 482.

remain under control of the British parliament. He made some significant changes to his earlier plan. He now accepted that New Brunswick was a province in her own right; the union would be composed of Nova Scotia with Prince Edward Island reunited to her, New Brunswick, Lower Canada and Upper Canada. More provinces could be created and provisional governments provided as required. The new state was less centralized than before; with the provinces retaining control over religion, law, land tenure, institutions and the administration of justice, and enabled to raise taxes. The provincial legislatures were restrained from enacting any legislation repugnant to the Grand Council of the Confederacy, composed as before of two houses. In giving greater power to the provinces he hoped to meet the criticism that a union would "extinguish" the provincial legislatures and be incapable of providing for local interests.[37]

His sympathy for the aspirations of French Canadians was even more marked. This was likely a consequence of the arrival in London of his son Norman with his latest tale of woe. The French Canadians, Uniacke wrote in anger, were "as much entitled to all the privileges of a British subject" as any of the English faction who thought they "might stand, as it respects them, in a degraded state".[38] In a general union New Brunswick and Nova Scotia would act as "umpires" between the feuding English and French in the Canadas.[39]

The report by the Nova Scotian council and assembly on the 1818 Anglo-American Convention had, for the first time, proposed a programme of public works to link British North America by land and water. Uniacke's seminal idea of "two great inland navigation systems" beginning at Halifax and linked by canals to the Bay of Fundy and across the Isthmus of Chignecto to the St. Lawrence and via the Ottawa and Rideau Rivers to the Great Lakes, was reiterated in his 1826 Observations. This link by navigable water was to be complemented by a military road from Fredericton to the Miramichi, and thence by a road along the lower St. Lawrence. Uniacke was the first British American to articulate the essential relationship between union and the necessity for means of communication to link the colonies and reinforce their political and economic interdependence.

The Observations were presented in manuscript form so that

---

37. This criticism was made by Brenton Halliburton in his pamphlet *Observations upon the Importance of the British North American Colonies to Great Britain by an Old Inhabitant of British America* (Halifax, 1825) p. 24.
38. Observations, 1826, p. 462.
39. Ibid., p. 468.

Bathurst could see them before publication. Uniacke told Bathurst he was prepared to encounter whatever opposition a public discussion on union might produce, but Bathurst was not even prepared to bring them before cabinet for fear of agitating a question that by 1826 seemed to have been put to rest.[40] The Observations were never published; the only public note they received was in the *New York Albion*, which reported that the British government had formed a plan for uniting the colonies into one confederate system.[41] His family retained a copy and when his son James Boyle, as one of the Nova Scotian delegates, went to confer with Lord Durham in 1838, he presented him with a copy.[42] Durham had arrived with the belief that federation of all the colonies should be attempted, but when he found that even the maritime colonies were opposed to this idea, he discarded it. Two generations, two rebellions, the threat of another invasion from the United States, and even greater factionalism in the political life of the colonies would pass before Uniacke's vision was consummated and his idealism justified that a new state would be founded on liberal principles and without violent revolution.[43]

At the behest of Wilmot Horton, Uniacke was called before the parliamentary Select Committee on Emigration which had been created to investigate the possibilities and general effects of emigration from Britain.[44] His testimony to the committee gave the most detailed and graphic descriptions of how settlement was carried out in Nova Scotia during the post-Napoleonic War wave of immigration. Although his idealistic vision of Nova Scotia and British North America caused him to make exaggerated claims about the availability of land and the ability to absorb immigrants, the British government was sufficiently impressed by his testimony that it despatched Colonel Thomas Cockburn to lay out 300,000 acres in Nova Scotia and New Brunswick for 10,000 immigrants. Cockburn was soon disabused about the feasibility of any such plan by Nova Scotians, and there was considerable embarrassment all around.

At the time Uniacke was giving his views to the parliamentary

---

40. Uniacke to Bathurst, April 29, 1826, CO 217, Vol. 146, P.R.O. and R.G. Trotter, *Canadian Federation: The Origins and Achievement*, p. 9.

41. Beamish Murdoch, *History of Nova Scotia*, Vol. III, p. 555.

42. R.G. Trotter, *Canadian Federation: Its Origin and Achievement*, footnote No. 11, p. 9.

43. Observations, 1826, p. 349.

44. His testimony is in *Report of the Select Committee on Emigration from the United Kingdom*, printed by order of the House of Commons, June 29, 1827. *The Novascotian*, October 19, 1826 carried an abstract of Uniacke's testimony to the committee.

committee, there was a major debate over the issue of government regulation of the deplorable conditions aboard emigrant ships. The British government had passed passenger acts in 1823 and 1825 to regulate conditions. However, previous to the acts, passage had been cheap enough so that the mass of emigrants financed their own passage. With the imposition of the acts, the cost had increased and in 1826 the flow of emigrants had dwindled. Uniacke was emphatic that emigration should be voluntary and the passenger acts repealed. In fact many of the Irish immigrants to Nova Scotia in this period were not coming directly, but via Newfoundland. As Uniacke explained, a poor man could come to Newfoundland in a fishing vessel as a "raw fisherman"; therefore the passenger regulations did not apply anyway. They left Newfoundland because of the system of employment in which their employer, according to Uniacke, "screws them down to almost nothing; he feeds them badly, and he pays them badly".[45] As a result they came to Nova Scotia, generally destitute, and became a burden on the province.

The pattern of Scottish emigration was different. The practice was for the "Scotchman" who had become habituated to life in Nova Scotia to return to Scotland as an adventurer to bring out passengers. He would travel through northern Scotland until he had recruited two or three hundred for whom he hired a vessel, took them out for a fee and generally made "something handsome for his trouble".[46] The increase in costs caused by the passenger acts had tended to put a stop to this tide of emigration. Uniacke was in no doubt that the acts "were calculated ... upon principles of humanity", but they had "operated directly the reverse of what the legislature intended, for it has kept people at home in a state of actual starvation, whose little means, if left to themselves to make use of, would have enabled them to escape from that state".[47]

Uniacke's opposition to the passenger acts was reinforced by the scenes of misery he found in Ireland during his visit in the summer of 1826. As he told Wilmot Horton, "Before I visited Ireland I had heard much of its misery and distress But no idea which I had formed came near the actual state in which I found it". The starvation, the evil of absentee land owners and the "desperate ferocity" had appalled him and reinforced in him the necessity for emigration. He had taken money collected by the Irish in Nova Scotia to give to their dear friends and relations so that they could emigrate; in return he had received "in

45. *Report of the Select Committee ...*, p. 46.
46. *Ibid.*, p. 71.
47. *Ibid.*, p. 38.

blessings and prayers from thousands the only return they had in their power to make for the trouble" he had taken for them.[48] The destitution of the Irish was so great that unregulated emigration was the lesser of the two evils. The passenger acts were repealed in 1827, but had to be re-enacted in 1828 because of the dreadful conditions that passengers had to undergo when there was no regulation. The experiences of unregulated immigration in 1827 caused the Nova Scotian assembly to pass an act requiring masters of ships to post a bond to pay for any passenger who became a public charge within one year by reason of disease or poverty.[49] Uniacke was the only Nova Scotian who believed in unregulated immigration into Nova Scotia. He had seen the misery of Ireland, but Nova Scotians saw only too well the misery of unregulated passenger shipping.

Uniacke's last voyage home did not meet his expectations. Bathurst's rebuff of his Observations must have wounded his pride and further disillusioned him that the British government would ever act to save her North American colonies from the fate he foresaw as inevitable. Nor had he been able to secure offices for his sons. But Horton had spoken of him in very complimentary terms in parliament and he could return at least with the knowledge his services would not go unrecognized if vacancies should occur.[50] Upon his arrival back in late 1827, he seems to have gone into near complete retirement. A year later he did accept the office of president of the Halifax Society for the Encouragement of the Fisheries. There was, however, some criticism that he was rarely in court; when this reached him he reacted with all his old energy and humour.

T.B. Akins, then a young lawyer and later British North America's pioneer archivist, related how, when sitting in court, he heard the creaking of shoes and the rustling of silk, and Uniacke appeared. Two prisoners were to be tried for grand larceny. Fortifying himself with a liberal pinch of snuff and speaking with a decided brogue, he addressed Judge Brenton Halliburton and the jury:

My Lord and Gentlemen of the Jury — You may perhaps be surprised to see the Attorney General, who rarely comes to court, here this morning; but I have

---

48. Uniacke to Wilmot Horton, August 1, 1826, CO 384, Vol. 17. P.R.O. By 1826 Uniacke had settled twenty-five Irish families on his estate in a community (no longer in existence) called Irish Town. They had arrived destitute and he supported them until they became self-subsisting.

49. See J.S. Martell, *Immigration To and Emigration From Nova Scotia*, Publication No. 6, P.A.N.S. (Halifax, 1942) pp. 23-4.

50. Crofton Uniacke to Sir George Murray, November 23, 1830, CO 217, Vol. 149, P.R.O.

come for the purpose of showing you that I am not that old horse turned out to grass that I have been represented to be.[51]

Then he asked for the indictment, and took over the case for the Crown. The prisoners were found guilty.

He no doubt enjoyed the occasion. His good humour turned to anger, however, when he discovered that both S.G.W. Archibald and Brenton Halliburton were conspiring behind his back to succeed to the chief justiceship. Blowers now wanted to retire and had corresponded with Sir Thomas Strange, now in India. Strange wanted to return to Nova Scotia and resume his old office. This arrangement did not materialize, but Blowers' desire seems to have become known. Archibald, as an intimate friend of Halliburton, encouraged him to seek the chief justiceship. Halliburton needed no encouragement and took Archibald into his confidence and showed him some of his private letters soliciting the appointment. Archibald, who still wanted the office himself, disclosed Halliburton's confidences to Uniacke.[52]

Uniacke seems to have been completely unaware that either Halliburton or Archibald would have the presumption to compete with him for an appointment that he believed would come to him by right. Like an elderly but still powerful lion, he engaged in battle. The three men met; Uniacke taxed Halliburton with Archibald's statements. Archibald, much embarrassed by his duplicity, denied the conversation. Uniacke was able to provide exact details of the time and place.

Uniacke immediately sent off memorials to the Colonial Office and to Sir James Kempt, now governor general at Quebec, stating his claim and disputing any claims that either of his competitors might have. He even enclosed an exchange of correspondence with Halliburton, who was now deeply worried that his reputation would be tarnished by a charge of intrigue. Uniacke told Halliburton that he was determined to become head of his profession and refuted any idea that he was either bodily or mentally incapable of assuming the chief justiceship. If he could not hold the office because of advanced age, he would resign, as he had "six sons who hold my character as the most valuable part of their inheritance and would soon prevent it from receiving the least stain".[53]

51. L.P. Power, "Richard John Uniacke", p. 110.

52. William Blowers Bliss to his brother Henry, October 20, 1829, MG 1, Vol. 1598, P.A.N.S. Bliss describes in some detail what apparently transpired.

53. Uniacke to Halliburton, October 19, 1829 enclosed in Uniacke to Sir George Murray. October 15, 1829, CO 217, Vol. 149, P.R.O. Although the letter to Murray is dated October 15, it was not dispatched until after the correspondence with Halliburton had taken place.

In England his son Crofton took up the case at the Colonial Office, attacking Halliburton for insulting "the last days of a venerable parent", while claiming that his father was "capable of labours which few men could endure". The Colonial Office seems to have given Crofton the papers relating to Halliburton's claim; Crofton said then that rather than have Halliburton succeed, he would himself give up his "flattering prospects" at the English bar and become chief justice of Nova Scotia.[54]

Even the dying Sir John Sherbrooke was brought into the fray by Halliburton and Uniacke, who asked him to enquire at the Colonial Office about Archibald's correspondence. He did this, apparently, but by mistake sent his reply to Archibald, to the consternation of the other two.[55] Archibald had been memorializing the Colonial Office for appointments but had not made clear that he really wanted the chief justiceship. Because of his non-residence he had been forced to give up the chief justiceship of Prince Edward Island and was in some financial difficulty. There was little sympathy for him; he had done better than most, considering that for a period of years he had held the chief justiceship as well as being solicitor general and speaker while carrying on a lucrative law practice. Once his "uncandid [sic] intriguing for promotion"[56] became general knowledge, he lost much of the respect of his friends and particularly those in the assembly. Even the radical Pictou *Colonial Patriot* took to denouncing him with nearly the same degree of abusive language that it was directing against members of the council.[57]

In the 1830 session of the assembly a dispute erupted between the council and the assembly over the revenue bills in which Archibald provided the leadership in the assembly that his critics had so long desired. In the ensuing election, called the Brandy Election, Archibald and his colleagues were vindicated by the voters. Contemporaries believed that the quarrel originated more in a clash of personalities

---

54. Crofton Uniacke to Robert Hay, November 17 and 23, 1829, CO 217, Vol. 149, P.R.O.

55. Israel Longworth, *Life of S.G.W. Archibald* (Halifax, 1881) pp. 52 and 92-3, Longworth uses as evidence an anonymous letter which appeared in *The Free Press*. The issues are no longer extant during the period when the letter presumably appeared.

56. Peleg Wiswall reporting to his wife a conversation he had had with Halliburton, May 28, 1830, MG 1, Vol. 980, No. 40, P.A.N.S.

57. *Colonial Patriot*, May 20, 1829 and March 27, 1830.

embittered by the competition for the chief justiceship than over constitutional principles.[58]

Relations had certainly deteriorated between the council and the assembly since the 1826 election. Few men could remember an election that had been more closely contested than in 1826. Nearly half the members returned had never sat in the assembly before,[59] but a number of these, such as T.C. Haliburton, the author of Sam Slick, Beamish Murdoch, the historian, and Alexander Stewart, an accomplished lawyer and merchant, were men of ability and more than prepared to challenge the council. And the council, which controlled almost all the patronage, used this power openly to punish and reward to gain support for its measures. The continued opposition of the council to the Pictou Academy and over marriage licences embittered many, but the right of the council to negate money resolutions sent up from the assembly drew the fiercest criticism, and for the first time since Governor John Parr's day there were calls for radical constitutional change. Haliburton had become the "orator" of the assembly, and the general mood was well expressed when he castigated the council as consisting of "twelve dignified, deep-read, pensioned old ladies, but filled with prejudices and whims like other antiquated spinsters".[60]

The council did not take kindly to Haliburton's caustic and censorious wit and he was forced to apologize. But there was much truth in his criticism. Blowers, although president of the council, exercised little leadership, finding at his age the task really beyond him. Michael Wallace, who after 1828 was often administrator in the absence of the governor and thus wittily called "King Michael", was over eighty. Uniacke attended the council regularly when the assembly was in session but otherwise was often absent. The leadership passed to a younger group, of whom Brenton Halliburton was the most prominent. Halliburton had never sat in the assembly and, with the exception of S.B. Robie, none of this younger group had done so or only for a short period. Competent, intelligent but presumptuous, Halliburton was alarmed at the "fiery harangues" emanating from the floor of the assembly. He attributed them to a faction playing on local and petty grievances which required the council to exercise a "cleansing control",

---

58. See William Blowers Bliss to his brother Henry, April 24, 1830, MG 1, Vol. 1599, P.A.N.S.; C.R. Fairbanks to Robert Hay, June 1, 1830, CO 217, Vol. 151, P.R.O., and Michael Wallace to Sir George Murray, May 10, 1830, CO 217, Vol. 150, P.R.O.

59. Draft of Beamish Murdoch's for his History of Nova Scotia, MG 1, Vol. 726, P.A.N.S.

60. *Novascotian*, Supplement, March 29, 1827.

and arrogantly believed that the council was "even more capable than Majorities" in the assembly to decide on legislation.[61]

Road appropriations were the one form of patronage available to the assemblymen, and the chaotic manner in which it was dispensed resulted in much abuse and gross inefficiency in the construction of roads. In Kings County, for example, there were in 1827 seventy-two road commissioners appointed to expend £470. Road commissioners often overspent on the quite illegal authority of individual assemblymen, who would turn up at the next session to haggle with their colleagues over making up the over-expenditure. Within the council no one tried harder than Uniacke to bring some order to the expenditures and he generally acted as council spokesman on roads in the conferences with committees of the assembly. He wanted more money spent on the major roads or "great roads" as they were called, but was not above having the Halifax-Windsor road altered to suit his convenience, as it passed by Mount Uniacke. In a tirade against members of the council, the *Colonial Patriot* told Uniacke to stick to prosecuting public delinquents and to do his own road-making. Probably written by McCulloch, the editorial compared Uniacke's "80 years of mental improvement" to that of a lobster.[62]

The 1830 session began no differently than its predecessors, but the haggling over road appropriations among members of the assembly and between the council and the assembly was more protracted than usual. Both bodies agreed on the total sum to be expended but within the assembly there seems to have been more than the usual disagreement on the division for each county, and there was considerable pressure to increase the total allocation to satisfy the demands of individual members and to appease the council, which wanted more money spent on the great roads. While trying to come to some agreement, the assembly suddenly discovered to its anger that a tax on foreign brandy had not been fully collected for three years because the collector of excise and member of the council, Hibbert Binney, had decided the tax was illegal. However, he had never informed the assembly.[63] The revelation provided an opportunity for the assembly to increase the revenue for road expenditures,

---

61. *Observations upon The Doctrine, Lately Advanced, That His Majesty's Council have no Constitutional Power to Control Individual Appropriations, or to Amend or Alter Money Bills . . . Pictou Academy* (Halifax, 1828). The pamphlet was undoubtedly written by Halliburton.

62. *Colonial Patriot*, January 9, 1830.

63. For the dispute between the council and the assembly and the Brandy Election, see Gene Morison, "The Brandy Election of 1830", *Collections*, N.S.H.S., Vol. 30, pp. 151-83.

while arguing that there was no increase in taxation, only the satisfactory collection of what was due.

The tax in question was 2s 4d on foreign brandy, gin and cordials, and of this amount only two shillings had been collected. The assembly act imposing the tax in 1826 had been poorly drafted but to the embarrassment of the assembly the error had not been noticed when the collector's accounts had been examined. Binney could not have acted as he did without legal advice, and that should have come from the law officers of the Crown, Uniacke and Archibald. However, the decision was made when Uniacke was still in England. Presumably Archibald's advice was not solicited. There is nothing in the council's records to show any order was issued to Binney, and the circumstances surrounding the order remain a mystery.

The assembly, which had already approved the revenue bills, amended them to include the additional four pence tax on brandy and sent them to the council just two days before the previous year's acts were to expire. The council appointed a committee of Uniacke, Robie and Enos Collins, the wealthy merchant, to confer with the assembly committee and instructed them to state that the duties should be reduced as they already were too burdensome on commerce. Further conferences ensued in which Uniacke was the principal spokesman but no agreement was reached. The council was prepared to accept all the revenue bills except the one imposing the additional four pence on brandy. Both the assembly and the council expected the other to back down but neither did, and the revenue acts expired at midnight on March 31st. Merchants such as Collins took full advantage and threw on the market their now tax free goods, which infuriated the assembly nearly as much as the actual rejection of the revenue bills.

According to the journals of the council the rejection of the revenue bills was unanimous, but Uniacke and Robie seemed to have been opposed.[64] Both had been on the committee that had negotiated with its assembly counterpart, and had argued the council's case with moderation. In 1822 the council had rejected two of the revenue bills and the matter had been resolved by conferences. Robie had been speaker then and he and Uniacke in 1830 had every reason to believe that there would be a similar outcome. When they realized late on March 31st that there

---

64. J.L.C., March 31, 1830. A letter from Mentor in the *Acadian Recorder*, June 12, 1830 remarks that "two of the oldest and most respectable of that Board [the council] (whether we consider the character of their offices, or the steady and conscientious discharge of public and private duties through the whole course of their lives) was opposed to the vote of rejection?". This seems to me could only refer to Uniacke and Robie.

could be no agreement, and after arguing against rejection, they presumably agreed to make the council's decision unanimous. Uniacke had twice presided as speaker when the council had acted in a similar way and on each occasion he had warned the council of its folly, while using his influence to moderate opinion in the assembly.

On April 1st the assembly sent a committee to search the council journals to determine what had happened the previous day. They reported back the next day that the council had rejected the revenue bills before the final conference, to try and resolve the issue. If correct, then the council could rightly be charged with duplicity. What had happened was that the clerk of the council had incorrectly recorded the sequence of events and although this was explained to the assembly committee, they chose to ignore the explanation.[65] The apparent duplicity of the council further angered the assembly, coming as it did upon the action of the merchants in flooding the market with duty-free goods and thus denying revenue to the treasury. The assembly passed a bill on the same day to revive the revenue acts containing the four pence tax on brandy. The council unanimously rejected the bill, arguing that the bill was in substance the same as the one already rejected and therefore it would be a violation of the rules of parliament to consider it again.

The second rejection caused Archibald to leave the speaker's chair and engage in the debate with an impassioned speech defending the constitutional right of the assembly to have the sole privilege of framing revenue bills. His speech was given extemporaneously, and the young Joseph Howe, who recorded it, toned down, or omitted, some of the more critical remarks directed at the council.[66] The speech roused the assembly and hardened its attitude. Only three members, one of whom was Uniacke's son Richard John, were prepared to defend the action of the council.

Within the council Archibald's attacks on it were seen as motivated by his falling out with Uniacke and Halliburton over the chief justiceship. Blowers, who by now must have been fully aware of the competition for his office, withdrew from the council in anger and disgust. The presidency passed to Uniacke, and he and Halliburton now assumed the leadership in making the council's case.

Uniacke was furious at the newspaper reports of Archibald's speech and those of others in the assembly reflecting in a "very indecorous

---

65. J.L.C., April 6, 1830.

66. William Blowers Bliss to his brother Henry, April 24, 1830. He remarks that Howe "softened down some of the speeches". John Barry in the assembly made the same charge in a letter to the *Acadian Recorder*, April 24, 1830.

manner" upon the council and the "scandalous and libellous charges" made against some of its members. The assembly was called upon to punish the members who had made the charges. He was particularly incensed, and with some reason, by the charge of duplicity levelled by Archibald. In this council message to the assembly written by Uniacke, the right of the council to reject the revenue bills was argued, concluding with one of Uniacke's literary flourishes that the "money of a British subject cannot be wrested from him at the will of a single Branch of the Legislature".[67] Constitutionally Uniacke was correct and this was recognized by one of the best legal minds in the assembly, J.W. Johnston.[68]

The debate continued in the assembly with Archibald's leadership becoming more pronounced, although his speeches became somewhat more moderate as he concentrated on constitutional arguments. In a shrewd move he justified his own intervention in the debate by referring to Uniacke's role as speaker in the 1799 appropriations dispute during Wentworth's governorship. He quoted from the assembly's resolution, which had been written by Uniacke, that it was the "sole inherent and inalienable right" of the assembly to originate money bills and one that "British subjects will never surrender but with their lives".[69] Under Uniacke's leadership the council was careful not to challenge this right, but to uphold the council right to reject the revenue bills, although it was conceded that this right was rarely used.

This was stated quite clearly in a council message sent to the assembly. The message, written jointly by Uniacke and Halliburton, went to the core of the dispute, which was the highly unsatisfactory way the assembly went about raising and appropriating the revenue. It charged members of the assembly in having a "personal interest" in increasing taxation and putting forward their "favorite" projects while supporting those of others to ensure the passage of their own.[70] Instead of careful scrutiny of appropriations, as took place in the House of Commons, the assembly showed little inclination to question the money resolutions of its members. Even the *Colonial Patriot* had criticized members for putting up resolutions well knowing that the council would quite justifiably reject them.[71] As a consequence, the council, backed by the Halifax mercantile community, had taken on itself to check taxation and to

---

67. J.L.C., April 7, 1830, Wrest means to wrench away something.
68. *Novascotian*, April 2, 1830. He believed the council had been ill-advised to reject the bills but suggested that the assembly should give way.
69. *Novascotian*, April 22, 1830.
70. J.L.C., April 12, 1830.
71. *Colonial Patriot*, May 20, 1829.

scrutinize appropriations to a much greater degree that it had done usually in the past.

The assembly had generally passively accepted the council's interventions, but by 1830 its opposition to the measures such as the Pictou Academy, favouritism to mercantile interests, blatant use of patronage and its increasingly arrogant attitude towards the assembly all combined to unite the assembly against it. Increasing criticism of the council throughout the province gave both reason and confidence for the assembly to challenge what it considered to be the unconstitutional behaviour of the council. When the assembly refused to take action against Archibald and other members for their supposed indecorous language, the council, acting on a resolution of Halliburton, refused to do any further business and advised Wallace as administrator to prorogue the session, which he did on April 13th.

Uniacke no doubt believed that the impasse could have been avoided if his ideas for constitutional reform had been implemented. His proposals to separate the council into executive and legislative bodies, to have members of the executive sit also in the assembly and to remove officials like Binney, the collector of excise, from the legislative process had all been rejected by his colleagues and the British government.

Until Archibald's speech he had been temperate and conciliatory, and had tried to resolve the issue, knowing better than anyone else the consequences of an impasse over money bills. He could readily accept that Archibald, as the first commoner, had a duty to defend the rights of the assembly as he himself had often done, but Archibald's personal attacks on council members broke the rules as he understood them. As Uniacke saw it, it was the duty of the speaker to ensure that proceedings in the house did not get out of control. When he had been speaker during the Wentworth years, he had never publicly attacked Wentworth or members of his council, but he had been no less forceful in upholding the rights of the assembly. Up to the 1830 session Archibald had played by the understood rules but for this reason had come under increasing criticism. His intrigue for promotion only compounded his difficulties. To Uniacke he chose to overcome them by demagoguery and that was unforgivable.

Nova Scotians were more politically aroused by the Brandy dispute than ever before and the papers were filled with comment and letters critical of the council. Uniacke did not escape criticism and one anonymous letter-writer accused him of "political delinquency".[72] As a

---

72. A letter by Omicron to Richard John Uniacke in the *Colonial Patriot*, August 14, 1830.

consequence of the death of George IV, the most violently contested election in the history of Nova Scotia was held, and friends of the council were soundly defeated. In the next session the revenue bills containing the four pence on brandy were passed in council without opposition.

Uniacke did not live to see the final outcome of the Brandy Election. He died on October 11th, 1830. He seems to have been in good health up to about two weeks before his death, as he did the spring supreme court circuit prosecuting cases for the crown with all his old vigour. Around the beginning of October he became quite ill, either with a chest or heart ailment. On the night of his death he still maintained the household routine of bestowing his blessings on his family, who stood outside his bedroom each night to receive them.[73] When he failed to appear for breakfast, his family went to his bedroom, and found that he had passed away peacefully in his sleep in his seventy-seventh year.

He had requested to be buried at the Mount, with simplicity, in the early morning in a blanket, with attendance only by his family, who were on no account to alter their dress. However, he was buried in the crypt of St. Paul's beside his beloved first wife and eldest daughter. Members of the Charitable Irish Society turned out in force to pay their last respects to their founder and president for many years.

Uniacke set out in his twenty-first year to seek his fortune in the New World and arrived by chance in Nova Scotia. After his brush with treason, he could have left Nova Scotia forever, but he chose to return filled with ambition to make his fortune and build a home for his family. He came to love his adopted land, and while his ambitions for himself and for his sons were never to be fulfilled completely, he did rise to be the most influential Nova Scotian of his day. In his mind he associated his own ambitions with those of a Nova Scotia whose destiny, he was convinced, was to be a great maritime state. This association did not go unnoticed by his contemporaries and engendered much bitterness at times. However, he was engaging in the struggle for patronage, as were his contemporaries, in an age when professional advancement and influence were dependent upon favour rather than upon votes. The democratic age created its own system of patronage, which Uniacke foresaw and dreaded.

His political philosophy can best be described as Burkean,

---

73. P. Lynch, "Early Reminiscences of Halifax", *Collections*, N.S.H.S., Vol. XVI, p. 191.

although Edmund Burke's concept of political parties acting upon principle was anathema to Uniacke. It was, however, his study of Blackstone that moulded his constitutional thinking. Blackstone's interpretation of the British constitution was rigid and legalistic, one in which the executive, legislative and judicial functions were clearly separated, with their rights and powers defined by immemorial practice. Blackstone did not describe the British constitution as it was, but as the law declared it to be. Even as Blackstone was writing, the prerogatives of the Crown were being eroded by the embryo development of the cabinet system with ministers responsible to parliament. By the 1820's Uniacke must have recognized the significance of these changes, but he chose to ignore them. His reason was probably that he believed they would enfeeble the executive hand of government. Such a development, if transferred to colonial governments, would in his view, have compounded their weakness of which he so disapproved.

Until the French Revolution, there was little philosophy underlying Uniacke's politics. Blackstone was his guide in constitutional matters and he was much absorbed in his struggle with his loyalist enemies. His main preoccupation was to stay alive professionally and politically. To do this, he had to develop and maintain his credibility as a loyal servant of the Crown worthy of advancement. That he was able to do so was no mean achievement, when it is considered that the full weight of the colonial Nova Scotian establishment was thrown against him. Professional advancement for himself and for his sons was never far from his mind, but this in itself does not explain the violence of his defence of the Church of England as the established church nor his fear of democracy. He could have remained a loyal servant of the Crown and used his influence to find ways to satisfy Dissenters, as he did for Catholics; instead he chose to oppose them with a vehemence that on occasion left him completely isolated. The fact of his opposition may be explained by ambition, but not the depth of his hostility nor the lengths to which he was prepared to go. This derived from his instinctive and philosophical antipathy to the vile heresies of atheism, republicanism and democracy; this antipathy grew out of his reaction to the French Revolution, and increased as he saw the spread of democracy to the "New America".

Uniacke's politics may then best be described as those of a moderate Tory in his constitutional views and an extreme Tory when it came to church and state. He was instinctively and philosophically a conservative. However, his was never a conservatism that simply defended the status quo, but was combined with the most prescient mind in British America; he saw that the status quo could no longer be maintained. The fetters that bound colonial trading had to be removed, the Procrustean colonial constitutions radically changed, and a great union of the colonies created.

What marks Uniacke out from his contemporaries in British America is not his bare union proposals themselves, but his vision of a great state rising in the northern half of the continent. It was he, more than anyone else, who recognized that the granting of commercial freedom would necessitate a new relationship between Britain and her colonies. Only through union and acceptance of a much greater degree of colonial independence and financial responsibility could this new imperial partnership be cemented in sentiment and reciprocal interests. No other British American, until the Confederation period, set out the destiny of the fledgeling and disunited colonies of British America in such detail and with such vision.

Contemporaries remembered Uniacke mostly for the sheer force of his personality. One, J.G. Marshall, saw him as "a most extraordinary and remarkable person" and wrote that he had not met Uniacke's equal in any of the many courts of law and parliaments he had visited.[74] His faith in Nova Scotia's destiny as a partner in a great empire was only to be equalled by Joseph Howe, who, in a more democratic age, would lead Nova Scotians to their greatest triumph, responsible government. Uniacke's fifth son, James Boyle, became the first premier under responsible government. Today Uniacke is best known for Mount Uniacke, visited by over 20,000 people a year, one of the historic properties in the province-wide complex operated by the Nova Scotia Museum. There the personality of a remarkable and extraordinary man still lives.

74. J.G. Marshall, *A Brief History of Public Proceedings and Events... with Province of Nova Scotia, during the earliest years of the present century* (Halifax, n.d.) p. 7.

Select Bibliography

Manuscripts

The official and family papers held by the Public Archives of Nova Scotia provided the main sources for Uniacke's public career and private life. The most important collection used was Record Group (RG) 1 which contains the state papers of the province, collected and catalogued by Thomas Beamish Akins. Other RG's used were RG 5, the papers of the legislative assembly, RG 36 and 39, court papers, RG 47, deeds and RG 8, the records of the Central Board of Agriculture.

The family and individual papers are in Manuscript Group (MG) 1 of the P.A.N.S. and the following were of particular use:

Uniacke Family Papers, MG 1, Vols. 926-7

S.B. Robie Papers, MG 1, Vol. 793

Peleg Wiswall Papers, MG 1, Vols. 979-80

Rev. Thomas McCulloch's Papers, MG 1, Vols. 550-8

White Family Papers, MG 1, Vol. 949

Wentworth Papers, MG 1, Vols. 970, 939-41

Bliss Family Papers, MG 1, Vols. 1598-99.

The official correspondence between governors and the Colonial Office as well as miscellaneous correspondence between individuals and the Colonial office are at the Public Record Office, London in the Colonial Office series 217-20. These are available on microfilm both at the P.A.N.S. and the Public Archives of Canada in Ottawa.

Other collections used were the Dalhousie Papers in the P.A.C.; Minutes and Papers of the Board of Governors of King's College in the King's College Library in Halifax, N.S. and Letters copied by Mr. C.E. Thomas on St. Paul's which can be made available through the P.A.N.S.

Newspapers

Newspapers proved to be an excellent source particularly after the Acadian Recorder began publication in 1813. Other newspapers of value were:

> The Nova-Scotian Gazette and Weekly Chronicle
> The Royal Gazette and The Nova-Scotian Advertiser
> The Free Press
> Colonial Patriot
> The Novascotian
> The Halifax Journal

Unpublished Theses and Manuscripts

The following Theses proved most helpful:

Butler, G.F., "Commercial Relations of Nova Scotia with the United States" (unpublished M.A. Thesis, Dalhousie University, 1934)

Martell, J.S., "Origins of Self Government in Nova Scotia, 1815-1836", (unpublished PhD. Thesis, University of London, 1935)

McMullin, S.E., "Thomas McCulloch: The Evolution of Liberal Mind" (unpublished PhD. Thesis, Dalhousie University, 1977)

Merrigan, Leonora A., "The Life and Times of Edmund Burke in Nova Scotia" (unpublished M.A. Thesis, Saint Mary's University, 1971)

Morison, M.G., "The Evolution of Political Parties in Nova Scotia, 1758-1848" (unpublished M.A. Thesis, Dalhousie, 1949)

Snowden, J.D., "Foot Prints in the Marsh Mud: Politics and Land Settlement in the Township of Sackville 1760-1800" (unpublished M.A. Thesis, University of New Brunswick, 1974)

Story, Nora, "The Churches and the State in Nova Scotia, 1749-1840: An Outline of Problems and Policy" (unpublished manuscript, Library of Public Archives of Nova Scotia)

Secondary Works

A Constitutional Friend, ed., *The Speeches of the Right Honourable Richard Brinsley Sheridan*, Vol. III (1842)

Archives, Public of Nova Scotia, *A Directory of the Members of the Legislative Assembly of Nova Scotia*, 1758-1958 (Halifax, 1958)

Atcheson, Nathaniel, *American Encroachments on British Rights*... (London, 1808)

Beck, J. Murray, *The Government of Nova Scotia* (University of Toronto Press, Toronto, 1957)

Blackstone, Sir William, *Commentaries of the Laws of England* (Philadelphia, 1771)

Bliss, Henry, *On Colonial Intercourse* (London, 1830)

Brown, Rev. Andrew, D.D., *The Perils of the Time and the Purposes for which they appointed. A Sermon, preached on the last Sabbath of the year 1794 and Published at the Request of the Hearers* (Halifax, 1795)

Burke, Edmund, *Letter of Instruction of the Catholic Missionaries of Nova Scotia and Its Dependencies* (Halifax, 1804)

Extracts from the proceedings of His Majesty's Council, February 21 & 28, 1788, in reference to complaints of improper and irregular administration of justice in the Supreme Court of Nova Scotia (Halifax, 1788)

Fergusson, C.B., *The Diary of Simeon Perkins, 1797-1803* (Champlain Society, Toronto, 1967)

_____, *The Diary of Simeon Perkins, 1804-1812* (Champlain Society, 1978)

Fingard, Judith, *The Anglican Design in Loyalist Nova Scotia 1783-1816* (S.P.C.K., London, 1972)

Froude, J.A., *The English in Ireland*, Vol. 3 (New York, 1874)

Graham, Gerald S., *Sea Power and British North America, 1783-1820* (Cambridge, 1941)

Haliburton, T.C., *A General Description of Nova Scotia* (printed at the Royal Acadian School, Halifax, 1823)

Halliburton, Brenton (attr.) *Observations upon the Importance of the British North American Colonies to Great Britain by an Old Inhabitant of British America* (Halifax, 1825)

_____, *Observations upon the Doctrine, Lately Advanced, That His Majesty's Council have no Constitutional Power to Control Individual Appropriations, or to Amend or Alter Money Bills; With A Few Remarks upon the Conduct of that Body on the Questions of granting Encouragement to Common Schools, and a permanent provision to the Pictou Academy* (Halifax, 1828)

Harris, Reginald V., *The Church of Saint Paul in Halifax, Nova Scotia, 1749-1949* (Ryerson, Toronto, 1949)

Hay, Captain W., *Reminiscences 1808-1815 under Wellington, Part II; Nova Scotia and Canada 1817-1823 with the Earl of Dalhousie* (London, 1901)

Hutchinson, Peter Orlando, *The Diary and Letters of His Excellancy Thomas Hutchinson, Esq.* (Houghton, Muffin Co., Boston, 1884)

Journals of the Legislative Assembly of Nova Scotia, 1758-1830

Kennedy, W.P.M., *Documents on the Canadian Constitution 1759-1915* (Oxford University Press, Toronto, 1918)

Kerr, W.B., *The Maritime Provinces of British North America and the American Revolution* (Busy East Press, Sackville, N.B., 1942)

Livermore, Shaw, *The Twilight of Federalism: The Disintegration of the*

Federalist Party 1815-1830 (Princeton University Press, 1962)

Longworth, Israel, *Life of S.G.W. Archibald* (Halifax, 1881)

MacNutt, W.S., *The Atlantic Provinces: The Emergence of Colonial Society 1712-1857* (McClelland and Stewart, Toronto, 1965)

Marshall, J.G., *A Brief History of Public Proceedings and events . . . in the Province of Nova Scotia, during the earliest years of the present century* (Halifax, n.d.)

————————————, *A Patriotic Call To Prepare in a season of Peace for One of Political Danger . . . by a Native of the Province* (Halifax, 1819)

Martell, J.S., "Government House", *Bulletin of the Public Archives of Nova Scotia*, Vol. 1, No. 4 (1939)

————————————, *Immigration to and Emigration from Nova Scotia 1815-1838*, publication, No. 6 (Public Archives of Nova Scotia, 1942)

————————————, "Richard John Uniacke" in RG Riddell, ed., *Canadian Portraits* (Oxford University Press, 1940)

————————————, *The Romance of Government House* (King's Printer, Halifax, 1939)

————————————, "A Documentary Study of Provincial Finance and Currency 1812-36", *Bulletin of the Public Archives of Nova Scotia*, Vol. II, No. 4 (1941)

————————————, "The Achievements of Agricola and the Agriculture Societies 1818-25", *Bulletin of the Public Archives of Nova Scotia*, Vol. II, No. 2 (1940)

Mayo, L.S., *John Wentworth: Governor of New Hampshire, 1767-1775)* (Harvard, 1921)

Murdoch, Beamish, *History of Nova Scotia*, Vol. III (Halifax, 1867)

Pares, Richard, *King George III and the Politicians* (Oxford, 1953)

Proceedings of the General Assembly upon the Convention Concluded between His Majesty and the United States of America (Halifax, June 1819)

Raymond, Rev. W.O., ed., *Winslow Papers, A.D. 1776-1826)* (St. John, N.B., 1901)

Report of the Select Committee On Emigration from the United Kingdom, printed by order of Parliament, June 29, 1827

Rives, George L., ed., *Selections from the Correspondence of Thomas Barclay (Harper Brothers, New York, 1894)*

Sabatier, William, *A Letter to the Right Honorable Frederick Robinson, President of the Board of Trade . . .* (London, 1821)

Schuyler, Robert Livingston, *The Fall of the Old Colonial System: A Study in British Free Trade 1770-1870* (Archon Books, Hamden, Conn., 1966)

Sykes, Rev. Norman, *Church and State in England in the XVIIIth Century*, reprint (Octagon Books, New York, 1975)

Trotter, R.G., *Canadian Federation: Its Origins and Achievement, A Study in Nation Building* (J.M. Dent & Sons, London, 1924)

Trueman, Howard, *The Chignecto Isthmus And Its First Settlers* (William Riggs, Toronto, 1902)

Uniacke, Richard John, *The Statutes at Large passed in the several General Assemblies held in His Majesty's Province of Nova Scotia . . .* (Halifax, 1805)

——————————, *The Attorney General's Answer* (Halifax, February 16, 1804) Appendix II to *A Charge Delivered to the clergy June and August 1803 by the Right Reverend Charles Inglis DD*, second edition (Halifax, 1801)

Ward, John Manning, *Colonial Self Government: The British Experience 1759-1856* (University of Toronto Press, Toronto, 1976)

Whitelaw, Marjorie, ed., *The Dalhousie Journals* (Oberon, c. 1978)

Whitelaw, William Menzies, *The Maritimes and Canada before Confederation* (Oxford University Press, Toronto, 1966)

Wise, S.F. and Brown, Robert Craig, *Canada Views the United States: Nineteenth - Century Political Attitudes* (Macmillan of Canada, 1967

Wright, Martin, *The Development of Legislative Council 1600-1945* (Faber, London, 1946)

Articles

Archibald, Sir Adams, "Life of Sir John Wentworth: Governor of Nova Scotia, 1792-1808, *Collections*, N.S.H.S., Vol. XX.

Burrough, Peter, "The Search for Economy: Imperial Administration of Nova Scotia in the 1830s", *C.H.R.*, Vol. 49, No. 1 (1968)

Butler, G.F., "The Early Organization and Influence of Halifax Merchants", *Collections*, N.S.H.S. Vol. 25.

Bulmer, J.T., "Trials for Treason", *Collections*, N.S.H.S., Vol. 1

Byrne, Cyril, "The Maritime Visits of Joseph Octave Plessis, Bishop of Quebec", *Collections*, N.S.H.S., Vol. 29.

Elliott, Shirley, "The Library of Richard John Uniacke 1753-1830, Attorney General of Nova Scotia", *Bulletin, Maritime Library*, Vol. 21, No. 2 (1957)

Ells, Margaret, "Nova Scotia Sparks of Liberty", *Dalhousie Review*, Vol. XVI, No. 4 (1937)

——————————, "Governor Wentworth's Patronage", *Collections*, N.S.H.S., Vol. XXV

——————————, "Clearing the Decks for the Loyalists", Canadian Historical Association, *Report* (1933)

_____, "Loyalist Attitudes", *Dalhousie Review,* Vol. XV, No. 3 (1935)

_____, "Settling the Loyalists in Nova Scotia", Canadian Historical Association, *Report* (1934)

Elwood, Marie, "Two Portraits attributed to Robert Feke", *The Magazine Antiques* (November, 1979)

Fitzgerald-Uniacke, R.G., "Some Old County Cork Families — The Uniackes of Youghal", *Journal of the Cork Historical and Archaelogical Society,* Vol. III, 1894, Nos. 30, 31, 33, 34, 35 and 36.

Gilroy, Marion, "The Partition of Nova Scotia, 1784", *C.H.R.,* Vol. 14, No. 4 (1933)

Graham, Gerald S., "The Origin of Free Ports", *C.H.R.,* Vol. XXII, No. 1 (1941)

Harvey, D.C., "The Intellectual Awakening of Nova Scotia", *Dalhousie Review,* Vol. 13, No. 1 (1933)

_____, "Uniacke's Memorandum to Windham, 1806", *C.H.R.,* Vol. XVII, No. 1 (1936)

_____, "History and Its Uses in Pre-Confederation Nova Scotia", Canadian Historical Association, *Report* (1938)

_____, "Nova Scotia and the Convention of 1818", Royal Society of Canada, *Transactions* (1933)

Hill, G.W., "History of St. Paul's Church, No. III, *Collections,* N.S.H.S., Vol. III.

Howe, Joseph, "Notes on Several Governors and their Influence," *Collections,* N.S.H.S., Vol. 17.

Jack, Daniel Russel, "An Affair of Honor", *Acadiensis,* Vol. 5 (1905)

Laing, Lionel H., "Nova Scotia's Admiralty Court as a Problem of Colonial Administration, *C.H.R.,* Vol. XVI, No. 2 (1935)

Lynch, P., "Early Reminiscences of Halifax", *Collections,* N.S.H.S., Vol. XVI

MacKinnon, Neil, "The Changing Attitudes of the Nova Scotian Loyalists to the United States, 1783-1791", *Acadiensis,* Vol. 2, No. 2 (1973)

_____, "The Enlightenment and Toryism: A Loyalist's Plan for Education in British North America", *Dalhousie Review,* Vol. 55, No. 2 (1975)

Martell, J.S., "Halifax During and After the War of 1812", *Dalhousie Review* Vol. 23, No. 3 (1943)

Martin, K.L.P., "The Union Bill of 1822", *C.H.R.,* Vol. 5, No. 1 (1924)

Murray, W.C., "History of St. Matthew's Church", *Collections,* N.S.H.S., Vol. XVI

Piers, Constance F., "Mount Uniacke, Colonial Seat of the Uniacke Family", *Canadian Homes and Gardens* (March 1927)

Ormsby, William, "The Problem of Canadian Union", *C.H.R.*, Vol. 39, No. 4 (1958)

Power, L.G., "Richard John Uniacke, *Collections*, N.S.H.S., Vol. IX "Proceedings of the House of Assembly", *The Nova-Scotia Magazine* (March and April, 1790)

Smith, William, "The Attempted Union of 1822", *C.H.R.*, Vol. 2, No. 1 (1921)

Story, Nora, "The Church and State Party in Nova Scotia, 1749-1851" *Collections*, N.S.H.S., Vol. 27

Sutherland, David, "Halifax Merchants and the Pursuit of Development, 1783-1850", *C.H.R.*, Vol. LIX, No. 1, (1978)

Vincent, Thomas B., "The Inquisition: Alexander Croke's Satire on Halifax Society during the Wentworth Years", *Dalhousie Review*, Vol. 53, No. 3 (1973)

Index

Sherbrooke, Sir John Coape, 65, 69, 75, 87, 88, 98, 126
Sheridan, Richard Brinsley, 29, 30
Slavery, 4
Smith, William, 108
Stanser, Bishop Robert, 98
Stephens, James, 68, 114, 115
Sterns, Jonathan, 17, 20, 25, 26, 35, 36
Stewart, James, 84, 99
Strange, Chief Justice Andrew, 21, 23, 25, 34, 125
Swayne, Major General, 65
Tonge, William Cottnam, 29, 39, 47
Tonge, Winkworth, 21, 22
Trade and Navigation Laws, 11, 52-3, 54, 65, 66, 67, 110, 113, 116
Twining, Rev. Thomas, 98, 99, 100, 101
Uniacke, origin of name, 2
Uniacke, Alicia, 63, 117, 119
Uniacke, Andrew Mitchell, 32, 105
Uniacke, Bartholomew, 4, 12
Uniacke, Crofton, 47, 64, 74, 75, 77, 119, 126
Uniacke, James (brother of Richard John Uniacke) 11, 47
Uniacke, James Boyle, 68, 117, 118, 122
Uniacke, Martha Maria, 5, 10, 12, 44
Uniacke, Norman (father of Richard John Uniacke), 2, 3, 4, 7, 45
Uniacke, Norman (son of Richard John Uniacke), 33, 36, 37, 44, 45, 49, 50, 77, 109, 110, 117
Uniacke, Richard John, 33, 42, 49, 64, 68, 69, 117, 120, 124; arrival in N.S., 1; birth, 2; attitude to religion, 2, 78-9, 134; Irish family, 2-4, 45; slavery, 4; marriages, 5, 44, 50; Cumberland Rebellion, 6-10, 26; Catholic emancipation, 11, 78, 81-3, 102-3; trade and navigation laws, 11, 52-3, 54, 65, 110, 115-6; appointment as solicitor general, 12; law practice, 12, 25, 33, 64; elections, 13, 18, 25, 37, 38-9; leader of pre-loyalists, 15, 16, 18-19, 21; advocate general, 16, 37, 52, 111; land granting, 16, 46, 70; as assemblyman, 17, 18, 37; impeachment of judges, 19-21; naval officer's fees, 21-2; as speaker, 21, 24, 37, 39, 40, 54, 130; money bills, 22-4, 37-8, 40-1, 61; 105-6, 128-32; duels, 26, 36; charged with disloyalty, 29-30; militia officer, 29, 30 and drafting of legislation, 60; Mason, 33; Charitable Irish Society, 13, 32, 102; appointment as attorney general, 26, 34-5; stories and anecdotes about, 31, 64, 65, 68, 69, 116, 124-5; influence of William Blackstone, 38, 134; promotion to council, 39, 60; 1806 visit and memoir, 41, 43, 47, 55-7, 59; Uniacke's Laws, 42, 52; conservative philosophy, 42, 81, 111-2, 133-5; Thomas Walker case, 47-8; destiny of N.S., 51-2; free ports, 53-4, 56, 58, 66; colonial union, 59, 66, 67, 107-8, 110, 120-1, 135; colonial constitutions, 59, 60, 66, 107-8, 135; council, separation of, 60,